Take the following quiz to find out.

How would you answer the following questions?

Your supervisor tells you that she wants to discuss your performance. Which of the following do you think?

a. You and your boss have different styles and you're pretty certain she'll be critical
b. You feel a sense of anxiety about the meeting come over you
c. You imagine you'll be complimented for all of your hard work—after all, good things come to hard workers
d. You mentally prepare a list of what you accomplished compared to your stated objectives from your last discussion and feel confident you've exceeded expectations

You've worked an entire day on an assignment for your boss only to discover that a co-worker failed to share a crucial piece of information with you. And you have to redo everything. Which of the responses below might describe how you'd deal with this situation?

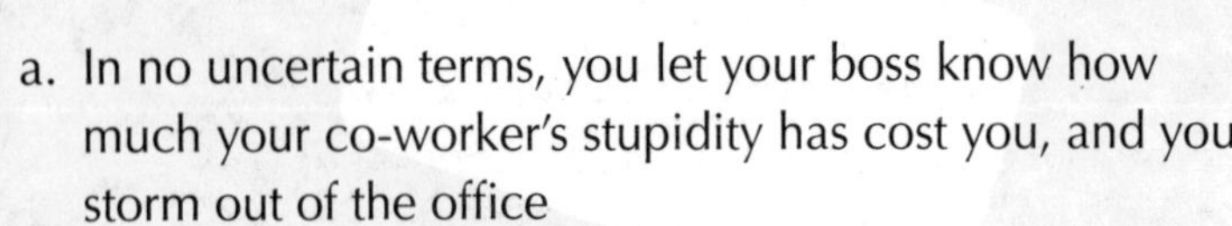

a. In no uncertain terms, you let your boss know how much your co-worker's stupidity has cost you, and you storm out of the office
b. You think to yourself, "This is exactly why I don't trust parts of my projects to others!"
c. You call your best friend and think how lucky you are to have someone to share your problems with
d. You take the annoying information for what it is, and stay at work until you get the assignment done

You're in a "no-idea-is-a-bad-idea" brainstorming session. What are you thinking?

a. You're in heaven—"Creative Thinker" is your middle name
b. You're terrified someone will ask you to suggest something
c. You like it when everyone works toward a shared goal
d. You're uncomfortable and feel like someone should soon steer the conversation to what all this means

Your spouse just lost her job, your kids have the flu, and a big project is due. What are you thinking?

a. There's almost nothing a couple of glasses of wine won't fix
b. You do what you've got to do, but make sure everyone knows how tough it is on you
c. You're glad you've got friends outside of work to support you at times like these
d. You make a plan—prioritize what needs to happen and ask for help when you need it

You walk into the employee's room and overhear a group of employees bad-mouthing one of your co-workers. What do you do?

a. You join in—it's important that you fit in on the job
b. You avoid the gossiping group
c. You distract people from the conversation, introducing a new topic
d. You stand up for the person

In general, which type of work environment suits you best?

a. An organization where ideas are debated publicly and the best ones win
b. A job where I know what's expected of me, and I'm given the time and resources to do it well
c. An organization that cares about employees' values
d. One in which decisions are made based on fact, truth, and numbers

• • •

As you imagined yourself in each situation, were you aware of what you were feeling? Anxious, angry, elated, frustrated, fearful, compassionate? Maybe you felt a combination of several emotions? If you were aware of your emotions, was your impulse to trust them, or try to override them with logic? Did different questions arouse different kinds of feelings? Do you know that those feelings contribute to your professional success or failure by consistently shaping the choices you make?

If you found that your answers fell predominantly into one category—more a's or c's, for instance—you'll discover in this book a set of diagnostic tools that I've developed—The Workplace Emotional Evaluation Profile—that precisely defines what those answers indicate about your individual emotional work style as well as your typical approach to handling emotional situations. But a diagnosis of your own emotional makeup is only one part of the emotional mastery equation—learning to identify and understand how *others* deal with emotion is nearly as important. *It's Always Personal* will help guide you, offering concrete strategies that will help you improve your skills at managing your own emotions and navigating your colleagues'.

Getting smart about emotion at work is not some airy-fairy luxury, rather, emotion management is an essential skill set for professional success. If you want to be more aware of those emotions and learn to channel them more productively, read on.

Praise for

IT'S ALWAYS PERSONAL

"Throughout this heartfelt book, Ms. Kreamer comes down on the side of accepting and expressing one's authentic feelings, though in sensible and constructive ways. *It's Always Personal* is not a manifesto for workplace encounter groups, but the book does argue that greater emotional openness could lend vitality to American business, and it urges both men and women to 'bring their full, true selves to the game.'"

—*The Wall Street Journal*

"*It's Always Personal* will transform the way you look at office culture and work relationships. In an insightful analysis packed with research, evidence, and real-life examples, Kreamer demonstrates why emotion matters so much in the workplace—and, with practical advice, she identifies ways to be happier and more effective at work."

—Gretchen Rubin, #1 *New York Times* bestselling author of *The Happiness Project*

"Anne Kreamer . . . has hit the 'It's about time!' button with her latest, *It's Always Personal: Emotion in the New Workplace.* Finally, someone is willing to unpack the morass of anger, anxiety, sadness, and joy that *drives the workday.* Yes, this bears repeating: drives the workday . . . what makes Kreamer's book transcend *Who Moved My Cheese*-yness is the tension that thrums beneath her ex-executive optimism and also her own still-palpable disappointment in the corporate sphere."

—*Elle*

"This will be one of the most fascinating and useful books you'll ever read. In this groundbreaking study, Anne Kreamer looks at emotion in the workplace through first-hand experiences, scientific research, and empirical data. What's the role of anger, fear, empathy, anxiety, and tears? This book explains them in ways that will make you a better worker, boss, and human being."

—WALTER ISAACSON, president and CEO, The Aspen Institute and former CEO of CNN

"Big girls do cry—and yell—at work, according to this lively, well-researched exploration of emotions on the job."

—*O: The Oprah Magazine*

"*It's Always Personal* made me want to stand up and cheer! I love this book. And every person who has ever been a boss or an employee needs to read it. Superb reading and highly practical!"

—CHRISTIANE NORTHRUP, M.D., *New York Times* bestselling author of *Women's Bodies, Women's Wisdom*

"Kreamer makes a solid case for her philosophy in the most compelling way possible . . . an extremely readable, well-reasoned volume."

—*Publishers Weekly*

"A magnificent book, deeply researched and fun to read, *It's Always Personal* is destined to become a classic in the field of men, women, and work."

—LOUANN BRIZENDINE, M.D., *New York Times* bestselling author of *The Female Brain*

"So what should be the rules and boundaries for showing how you feel while you work? That's a question asked and answered in Anne Kreamer's fascinating book."

—*The Washington Post*

IT'S ALWAYS PERSONAL

BY ANNE KREAMER

It's Always Personal: Navigating Emotion in the New Workplace

Going Gray: What I Learned about Beauty, Sex, Work, Motherhood, Authenticity, and Everything Else That Really Matters

IT'S ALWAYS PERSONAL

NAVIGATING EMOTION *in the* NEW WORKPLACE

Anne Kreamer

RANDOM HOUSE TRADE PAPERBACKS / NEW YORK

It's Always Personal is a work of nonfiction. Some names and identifying details have been changed.

2012 Random House Trade Paperback Edition

Published in the United States by Random House Trade Paperbacks, an imprint of The Random House Publishing Group, a division of Random House, Inc., New York.

RANDOM HOUSE TRADE PAPERBACKS and colophon are trademarks of Random House, Inc.

Originally published in hardcover and in slightly different form in the United States by Random House, an imprint of The Random House Publishing Group, a division of Random House, Inc., in 2011.

ISBN 978-0-8129-7993-0
eBook ISBN 978-0-679-60493-8

Printed in the United States of America

www.atrandom.com

2 4 6 8 9 7 5 3 1

Book design by Casey Hampton

For Kate and Lucy

Let's not forget that small emotions are the great captains of our lives. —Vincent van Gogh

Contents

IT'S ALWAYS PERSONAL

ONE

The Moment of Truth

Experience is not what happens to a man, it is what a man does with what happens to him. —Aldous Huxley

Late in the day, May 18, 1993, I was celebrating the completion of a very important piece of business with a few colleagues in my high-rise office in Times Square, right in the electric center of Manhattan. I was a 37-year-old senior vice president, heading the consumer products and publishing division of Nickelodeon, the children's cable channel, and we'd just announced a huge, unprecedented deal with Sony to create and market home videos of hit Nickelodeon shows such as *Rugrats* and *Ren & Stimpy.*

My team and I were experiencing that rush of euphoria, the physical high when endorphins flood the body after the competition is won, a test aced, an adversary outmaneuvered. Getting the deal done had been stressful, filled with tough meetings, late nights, and frayed nerves—and *sharing* in the glory of the moment of triumph further heightened our sense of accomplishment. Like teammates obsessively rerunning the game films of our championship season, each of us took a turn recounting different pieces of the story, weaving our collective insiders' tale of the Great Deal by reliving the emotional ups and downs of the previous eighteen months.

"How many business models do you think we ran? A hundred?"

"A *million.* If I ever hear the words 'sell through' again I'll scream."

"Or 'stock keeping unit.' "

"Do you remember management grilling us on our P&Ls? It was like the Inquisition!"

"And the look on those guys' faces at Disney when we told them sorry, but $18 million just wasn't good enough! Damn, that felt great!"

We convulsed with laughter when a junior team member perfectly imitated the way a certain big-name lawyer had waddled shoeless around his office during some of our meetings.

Maybe our repartee was not the stuff of legend, but the experience of creating and closing the deal had enriched personal connections that we wanted to savor. We were giddy, simultaneously exhausted from the countless negotiating hours and ecstatic from finally finishing it. No matter how trivial the recollection or joke, we were members of a troupe performing for one another, and it felt great. It was a go-go time in the country and a *seriously* go-go time at Nickelodeon, then just twelve years old. We were the zeitgeist. We were the champions. And if you've ever closed a big deal or helped build an up-and-coming organization, you know how we were feeling. Golden.

The phone rang.

My assistant shouted out, "Oh, *man*—it's *Sumner*! On line one!"

That's Sumner as in Sumner Redstone, then as now the chairman and majority owner of Viacom, Inc., the parent company of

Nickelodeon. During my three years at the company Redstone had rarely spoken to me, and had never phoned.

I gaily answered. *How generous of Sumner,* I thought, *to take the time and make the effort to thank me personally. Now* that's *a good boss.* This was it. My personal moment of glory.

I eagerly picked up the phone, anticipating verbal high-fives, a congratulatory exchange about what a great job we'd done. Instead, Redstone, at that moment nine days shy of 70 years old, started screaming at me.

What?!

I was absolutely blindsided, sucker punched. I hunched over the telephone, turned my back on my colleagues, and gazed, unseeingly, at the high-rise across the street.

My vision narrowed and no ambient sound penetrated my hearing as Redstone's rant seemed to magnify in intensity and reverberate throughout my brain and body. I felt my heart racing. My head got that muffled sense of being stuffed with cotton. My palms, which never sweat, moistened. He was the lion and I was the prey. It became an out-of-body experience, as I watched my quivering, helpless self from above.

Redstone wasn't delivering strategic or tactical criticism, but rather *personally* attacking me. I could practically feel his spittle frothing out of my telephone receiver. I sat there supremely disappointed in being so undervalued for my many months of hard work and mortified to feel tears welling up while colleagues were in my office.

And the cause of his rage? In spite of healthy media coverage, including a positive piece in *The Wall Street Journal,* the public announcement of the Sony deal had failed to make Viacom's stock price move up.

Unbeknownst to me and most of the world, Redstone was at that time planning a hostile takeover of Paramount Communications—a takeover that he in fact consummated nine months later—and it was thus essential to him that his currency for the acquisition, Viacom's stock, rise in value quickly and significantly. But how could I have known that the announcement of Nickelodeon's home-video deal with Sony had been expected to push up the share price? I was an executive in a division within a division of the parent company. Perhaps my bosses knew of this high-stakes expectation, but I certainly didn't. And even if I *had* known, how and why could *I* be held responsible for how the stock market responded? As important as the deal was for Nickelodeon, in the overall scheme of Viacom's annual revenues ($1.9 billion in 1993), our $25-million deal was extremely modest.

Redstone continued in full-on attack mode. "Do you know what you've *done*?" is the one line I remember from the tirade. Mainly it was his vituperative rage that registered in my mind. There was no pretense of civility, let alone reasonableness. I kept mumbling apologies: *I'm so sorry, sir. I had no idea.*

I was startled *and* incensed. My anger at the injustice of being singled out for abuse made me feel like exploding. But I couldn't. To express what I was really feeling would have been professional suicide. I had no doubt that he'd have fired me on the spot. Instead, as I was outwardly groveling, I had a parallel conversation running in my head: "WHAT DO I HAVE TO DO WITH ANY OF THIS? GET OUT OF MY FACE, YOU IMPOSSIBLE OLD MAN! YOU DON'T UNDERSTAND ANYTHING ABOUT ANYTHING!" But you know what? Interior monologues aren't very emotionally helpful.

Less than ninety seconds after I'd happily picked up the phone, Redstone, without a good-bye, hung up. The viciousness of the assault and the suddenness with which he ended it were breathtaking. In shock and frustration, having been too stunned and scared to defend myself, the tears that had begun to well up during the call spilled out, as I tried to process the information. *Was* I at fault? *Had* I done something wrong? Why *hadn't* anyone told me how critical Redstone considered the deal? What could I have done differently?

I was physically shaking with the anger that I felt but could not safely or appropriately express, and my body understood that I had to expel that anger somehow . . . so I cried. *Bam!* Just like that. In less than two minutes I'd gone from feeling on top of the world to feeling like scum on a pond—and, worse, a specific pathetic subspecies, *crying female* scum.

If I had been alone in my office during the call, I surely would have really sobbed, letting it all out, discharging my feelings, then gotten up, gone home, had a glass of wine (or two or three), vented to my husband, relieved some of my pain, and moved on. Because I'd teared up in front of my team I was embarrassed, and felt like I had to bottle up my feelings. Being yelled at or feeling intense anger or crying in public is tough enough to deal with on its own, but the trifecta felt exponentially humiliating. I wiped my eyes and while my roiling emotions—shock, anger, anxiety, fear, and sadness—warred within, I had only the nanosecond it took to swivel my chair back to face the group to decide how I should present Redstone's call to them. On one hand, I wanted their sympathy and support. What right did that removed-from-reality jerk have to lambaste me? To bolster my just-battered self-esteem I craved the team's who-does-he-think-he-is? outrage on my behalf, on our behalf. But it wasn't such an easy decision. I worried that I might lose face. I was also concerned that while I might feel better if they rallied around me, the only thing I'd accomplish if I shared Redstone's anger would be to make them upset, too. Did I really want them to think that all of their sacrifices—their late nights, long business trips, and stress—were wasted? No way. I was their boss. Both to shore up my sense that we had done a good job and to shield the team from feeling discredited, I casually swiped my tears away and decided to pretend like the call was no big deal.

I have no recollection of what happened next because specific details from those moments have been lost to me in the haze of post-traumatic stress. Fearing a total meltdown, I recollect that with a wobbly smile I avoided saying anything detailed about the call, managing, perhaps, to force out an uninspired, "Great job, everyone! I am suddenly so tired I can hardly hold my head up. How about we call it a day and all go home?" I had no ability to fake it any further and needed to be alone. And fast.

You'd think a fifteen-years-in-the-workforce executive would have been toughened up and more cynical about work—who among us hasn't had a boss unjustly snarl or shout at us?—but it wasn't until the day after the call that I fully appreciated that my work was really, finally, just a job. Up to then I'd felt like a member of the A-Team, part of one of those splendidly serendipitous confluences when a few very lucky people with a shared vision and the resources to realize their dreams happen to be in the right place at the right time. Only after the call did I viscerally understand that our mission was not to make the world a better place for kids, it was to produce a momentary uptick in a stock price. I was merely one teensy machine part that could be capriciously ripped out, smashed, and discarded. That perhaps naive-seeming epiphany, that tiny isotope of grievance—*I'm killing myself for this kind of treatment?*—began to metastasize over time.

Two years, seven months, and fifteen days after I cried at work, I quit, without a new job.

In the scheme of things was what I experienced that afternoon really such a big deal? No. Was Redstone's anger at me legitimate? No. Was crying my only option? For me it was. Should I have felt even worse because I did cry? No. Did Redstone make it personal? Yes. Did I take it personally? Yes.

But let's widen the scope of those questions beyond my case. Is it a real problem that while emotion underlies nearly all important work decisions, most of us most of the time pretend that it's not so? Yes. Is it a problem that we remain clueless about why and how emotion drives work, and about how we should handle it? Absolutely. Might someone else handle a similar situation differently? You bet.

Take the case of Cyndi Stivers, the managing editor of *Entertainment Weekly*'s EW.com. On paper she and I are similar. We both started working in the late seventies, part of the second major modern wave of women to enter the labor force, and we have both worked in a variety of different areas of the media. But we are very different in our operating styles.

While I like to believe that at my core I'm a relatively even-keeled person, the truth is that it is always a huge effort for me to project outward calm. My emotions, both good and bad, always run close to the surface. I regularly tear up reading stories of personal sacrifice in the paper and even when watching treacly television commercials celebrating our shared humanity. I become overtly enthusiastic when good ideas emerge during brainstorming sessions or when someone does their work exceptionally well. To me, these are good qualities—ones that make me empathetic and fuel my creativity. But the flip side of this sensitivity and openness is that I also tend to obsess about slights or problems that would be insignificant to others, a stewing-over-everything quality that makes me vulnerable to feeling overly agitated by the inevitable ups and downs of everyday life. While this thin skin can sometimes interfere with my effectiveness, my preoccupation with how others view me also inspires me to consistently try to do my best. So who is to say what level of emotional sensitivity is optimal? I believe that I was born sensitive and that that's neither a good thing nor a bad thing in and of itself. It's simply part of who I am.

What *was* an almost insurmountable challenge for me as an executive, I now know, was my sense that my sensitivity was something negative in the context of work, something weak and inferior in me that should be subverted or conquered. Consequently, the whole "man-up" bravado that I felt was required of me on the job became a chronic and ever-increasing source of stress during the fifteen years I rose through the ranks. The "work" of acting like a manager often felt more challenging to me than the work itself. Whenever I walked into the extremely extroverted, game-on! MTV Networks culture, a hard-partying, cowboys-making-up-the-rules-as-we-went-along, the-more-outrageous-the-idea-the-better office environment, I felt like I had to put on my game face. I developed an artificial persona of a tough-talking, hard-drinking executive. Which meant, in other words, that I forced myself to act more like a guy.

Cyndi, on the other hand, seems to thrive in a variety of different kinds of work situations, always projecting a seemingly effortless level of calm and, unlike me, she doesn't seem prone to chewing over possible slights. While I'm certain she deals with extremely high levels of anxiety, from my perspective she could be the poster girl for the unflappable executive. Unlike my perpetual state of personal/professional personality dissonance, Cyndi also seems to have no difficulty reconciling her professional and private selves. At work or at a party, she radiates an optimistic attitude that is in sync with her cheerful exterior. Her appearance, particularly when she was younger—a turned-up nose, apple cheeks, and dimples—would often make people in work situations dismiss her as unserious. But it's more than just appearance—Cyndi projects the aura of a person with a high internal set point for happiness. In the same way I believe that I was born sensitive, Cyndi says, "I am hardwired to be cheerful." And she turned her naturally upbeat disposition to her advantage, discovering that "there is strength and resilience that some may not expect. And I guess because I'm a WASP, I'm not a big crier."

To demonstrate her even-keeled nature, Cyndi recalled a time when she felt challenged. Fairly early on in her career, as she was discussing the ins and outs of a new job for a competing magazine over lunch at the UN Plaza with her former boss and mentor, Clay Felker (founder of *New York* magazine and former editor of *Esquire* and the *Village Voice*), Cyndi benefited from valuable professional advice from an unusual source. "To my surprise," she says, "John Travolta came over to our table to say hi. Clay had commissioned the *New York* cover story that became *Saturday Night Fever,* Travolta's big break. It turned out that Travolta knew the prospective boss at my new job well, too, so I asked if he had any advice for me—a throwaway question, but he took it seriously. He got quiet for a minute, and then said, 'What you need to know about that guy is, he is going to lie in wait and look for where you are vulnerable, and one day when you are at your weakest, he's going to pluck that chord to prove his mastery over you.' "

Six months after starting the job she'd been discussing with Felker, Cyndi's new boss did exactly what Travolta had warned her about—and being forewarned definitely forearmed her. "I walked into a meeting to get a sign-off on cover lines," she said. "The room was full of men, and as soon as I walked in the door, I could smell that the editor in chief had had a liquid lunch. A quick glance at the guys around the table told me that it hadn't been going well for them, either—I got flashes of pain, concern, warning, as if they wanted to say, 'Oh, no! Bad time to try to do this!' " At the time Cyndi didn't know any of her male colleagues very well, but she instinctively knew they were all comrades facing the vicissitudes of working for such a mercurial character. "Once I realized the boss was in an ornery mood," she said, "I was on alert—and it only took a second or two to flash back to Travolta's advice and realize what was about to happen. Apologizing for the interruption, I handed the guy the sheet of cover lines. He scanned it, then tossed the paper back at me and bellowed, 'You call these cover lines? Go back to J school!' "

Cyndi thought, "Okay, this is the part where he tries to make me cry." The guys around the table looked terrified. But she realized she could defuse the situation with a joke. "Actually," she reminded the boss, startling the other men in the room, "I didn't go to J school. And as I recall, *you* didn't, either." After a beat, "one of the guys started chuckling, and then the boss did, and then everyone roared with laughter. Suddenly it was all comical. 'Get the fuck out of here,' he growled, now playfully. And he never picked on me again." By not backing down and instead responding with her characteristic humor, Cyndi successfully avoided a potentially emotionally fraught exchange and leveled the playing field with her occasionally nasty boss.

"For some reason, in such situations," Cyndi says, "I tend to stay very calm and analytical. I save my emotional reaction for afterward. I knew he didn't really mean it—and I also instantly sensed that I could probably jolly him out of it." Cyndi's found that if you can keep your presence of mind and crack a joke or two, it can snap a whole room out of a tense situation, particularly if the stakes are as low as they were here. "And I knew this guy wouldn't want to seem humorless in front of those other men."

Was Cyndi's boss's anger justified? No. Was his criticism, like Redstone's, meant to be personal, to wound? Yes. Was Cyndi's quick comeback *better* than my tears? Not necessarily. Cyndi's pithy response to an irate boss out for blood—neither yelling in kind nor crying—could not have been more different from my tears. But humor isn't for everyone and can also misfire. One could easily imagine her boss, who had been drinking, becoming enraged by being one-upped in public by a young woman. What is important is that Cyndi read the mood of the room and responded both authentically and shrewdly—with her usual upbeat approach.

It's Always Personal explores these differences in our individual emotional wiring and through a deeper exploration of the six primary workplace emotional flashpoints—anger, fear, anxiety, empathy, happiness, and crying—offers a blueprint for how each of us can remain true to our individual temperament while nevertheless developing the means to be more effective within the social context of work. In this book I hope to demonstrate a proposition that at first seems like an oxymoron—that we can get *rational* about our emotions, especially at work. By this I don't mean that we pretend that what we are feeling when embarrassed, frustrated, or upset at work isn't important, but rather that we learn to interpret *why* those particular feelings were triggered, understanding what happened on a psychological and even biological level.

> *What is essential is invisible to the eye.*
>
> —Antoine de Saint Exupery

The particular elements of jobs vary widely. The skills a waiter uses to handle a rowdy party of eight, for instance, are very different from those an engineer uses in developing a wind farm or those an entrepreneur uses to start a home design-consulting business. But from occupation to occupation and workplace to workplace, the underlying human fabric—the web of *interpersonal* connection and conflict—is similar. Emotions are omnipresent in our work, even though work and emotion are rarely discussed and analyzed together, but rather as if they existed in strictly separate worlds.

Emotions don't turn on and off like a tap—they are multidimensional, more like a revolving 3-D double helix than a simple *x/y* graph. Emotions are slippery, changing from moment to moment and office to hallway, according to permutations of gender, ethnicity, education, and age. They're how we balance empathy with dollars-and-cents business directives. They shape the cultural norms of an organization. They drive competition or collaboration. They are the worries or thrills that wake you up in the middle of the night or the opportunities that get you out of bed in the morning.

Emotions also operate like rivers—sometimes a river runs smoothly, sometimes broad and slow, sometimes narrow and fast, sometimes straight and sometimes with zigzagging switchbacks, with invigorating or terrifying rapids and with eddies and backwaters. Emotions can be ignored or dammed up and then spill over in a disastrous flood. We can, however, engineer and guide their course so that they flow productively—used, if you will, for irrigating our crops and generating our power. The trick is in learning to understand that emotions are idiosyncratic—that what works to keep one person's emotional river running smoothly will be different from what works for another.

All human relationships are complicated, and those at work, where we spend the majority of our adult waking hours and where our livelihoods hang in the balance, are often especially so. One way to help keep the river running is to understand that working entails a human reciprocity that involves not only how we are viewed by people who range from strangers to friends—colleagues, bosses, underlings, suppliers, vendors, partners, clients, customers, competitors—but also, equally important, how we view them. We have very little ability to control many of the circumstances that affect us at work—vacillations in the economy, an irrationally panicked buyer, the IT system crashing, an SOB coworker, a competitor's brilliant move. The context and timing of any situation influences the intensity or duration of our emotional response and how we might respond. Our reaction to the office clown joking about a recent oversight over lunch is very different from what we might feel if the boss made a big deal of a late report during a company meeting. But each of us does possess the power to shape how we *choose* to respond to those circumstances—to slide around the boulder in the stream rather than pound against it. We really do have the ability to control what we allow to upset us and to manage how we react. To acquire that personal mastery, it is essential that we understand and think about emotion specifically in the context of work, and do so in fresh ways.

Real emotional intelligence is more than just being sensitive or "nice," more than understanding how to read the mood of a conference room or having insight into whether a colleague is more analytical or expressive in her approach to problem-solving. While those are important skills, effective emotional knowledge demands a profound level of *self-reflection,* an active imagination, and an ability not only to envision alternate approaches to a given situation but also to understand that there are entire invisible galaxies of salient emotional facts behind almost every workplace exchange.

Sigal Barsade, an expert on emotion within organizations and a professor at the Wharton School of Business at the University of Pennsylvania, puts it this way, "People don't come to the workplace [with a] tabula rasa. Rather they have a prior life and work history that can influence their thoughts and behaviors on the job. Traditionally, organizational behavior has only examined things people could easily see or report. But I think we've missed an entire level of analysis, which is unconscious. For instance," Barsade says, "if a man is cut off in traffic on his way to work and then has to make a strategic decision in a 9 a.m. meeting, if I were to ask him if the anger he felt during the traffic encounter in any way influenced his later strategic decision, he'd answer 'absolutely not,' when we have concrete evidence that it would. We are unaware of how diffuse our moods are, and this lack of awareness can be insidious."

But if you think that dealing with the emotional nuances, contexts, and subtexts *and* getting your job done sounds daunting, you're not alone. We're all working 24/7 with half the resources and twice the hurdles. And really, when your boss needs the presentation *ASAP,* how much more sensitive can you possibly be? Adding another layer of responsibility, having to worry about what you're feeling, let alone what everyone around you may be feeling, takes us off task, away from the nitty-gritty of work. It's one more thing to deal with, to fail at, and can feel like a bridge too far for things we need to improve about ourselves. Who has the time? Or the energy? It seems easier to tuck our heads down and take care of business, narrowly defined.

In fact, because we almost never discuss and don't understand how emotion works at work—because we aren't thoughtful about emotion—we sabotage ourselves, neither understanding how to cultivate our most effective behaviors nor how to mitigate our worst. If you've ever spent more time cleaning up a mess after what seemed like a relatively minor confusion about the intent of an assignment than the time spent on the assignment itself, you know what I mean.

I'm not suggesting you adopt some fake version of touchy-feely "active listening," the rote "what I hear you saying . . ." kind of thing. Often that kind of forced empathy rings false. What I *am* talking about is a deeper level of self-knowledge informed by recognizing what makes your warning signs flash, what drives you crazy, what makes you feel sick with worry, so that you can learn to anticipate trouble *before* it strikes.

When you can consistently and successfully predict how you will respond to the behavior of certain colleagues in certain predictable situations, and how they will respond to your individual style, then you can develop appropriate skills to proactively deal with the things that push your buttons. And because we're human, when you inevitably end up blowing a gasket, you'll be able to mitigate the damage by being able to explain what happened to yourself and the other people involved.

This approach would have been of great help to me when I managed others and was managed in the workplace. The kind of coaching that I received at the time focused primarily on ways I had to *change,* to be a different person in order to be a better executive—be less demonstrative, be less spontaneous, be a better listener, be someone I really wasn't. I'm suggesting that we learn to tolerate a far greater range of emotions at work, for both women and men. Being honest about how you tick will allow you to feel more comfortable in your skin and help you become more successful. To be human is to be emotional. And in spite of how often difficult workplace exchanges are prefaced by the "please don't take this personally, it's just business" platitude, it's never *just* work. Our senses of identity and self-esteem are closely bound to our jobs—especially if we're lucky enough to have a job we care about.

Fortunately, we live in a pivotal historical moment in which we have new resources to help us learn how to understand what precipitates our emotional states and, based on that scientific understanding, how we can better manage them. During the last couple of decades, through the use of functional magnetic resonance imaging (fMRI)—a measure of the flow of blood in living brains by neuroimaging scanners—scientists have accessed the inner workings of actively engaged minds as never before. Now we are beginning to understand exactly *why* and *how* men are from Mars and women are from Venus. Advances in neurobiology have begun to reveal that while the genders may be roughly equal in basic intelligence, the ways that each gender tends to learn, process, and distribute information and react emotionally tend to be quite different. Yet nearly four decades into an era of empowered women and dual-gender workplaces, the differences between women and men remain a subject as undiscussed and off-limits as it is large and important. It is a gigantic elephant in the room, akin to the situation regarding female sexuality in Victorian times. Women are equal to men, but emotionally they are manifestly not the same as men.

So this is something else I'm hoping to explore in this book: Can the rules of conduct for work life be rethought and remade to accommodate—and to *use,* productively—the neurobiological and cultural differences between men and women? And can this be done without over-worrying that we're violating PC taboos by even bringing up the subject—and without sacrificing the hard-won progress toward fairness and equality? We are a society and culture confused and in flux on this issue at a moment when, suddenly, as of 2010, for the first time in our history, more American workers are female than male.

Women's new workforce majority is just one of many metrics of twenty-first-century female professional and economic empowerment. Women today account for 57 percent of college and university undergraduates and 62 percent of graduate students, and in a very few decades women have gone from being 6 percent of doctors and 3 percent of lawyers to the majority of those graduating from medical and law schools. Despite the continuing rarity of women at the very tops of large corporations and in finance, a 2004 study by the women's business group Catalyst, *The Bottom Line: Connecting Corporate Performance and Gender Diversity,* concluded that companies with the highest percentages of women in their executive ranks achieved 35 percent higher returns. What's more, according to the Center for Women's Business Research, women today own 40 percent of the private businesses in the United States. And traditional resistance to the male-to-female power shift also seems to be softening, if not disappearing: according to a 2009 *Time* magazine poll, 76 percent of Americans view female economic parity as a positive trend for society, and 80 percent view women in the workforce as positive for the economy.

Daniel Goleman, author of the seminal book *Emotional Intelligence,* and the godfather of the EQ movement, concurs that a shift is under way. "What's changing," he says, "is how we are socialized in emotion, which traits are valued or devalued because cultural norms shift with historic trends. And because women do experience and express emotions more freely, it makes sense that as women occupy more positions of power the expression of emotion in the workplace will become more acceptable." I believe that these profound social changes, in tandem with the new scientific insights into the ways each gender operates, will transform the future of interpersonal dynamics on the job and create unprecedented opportunities to look with fresh eyes at the ways in which people interact and express feelings at work.

TWO

Emotion 101

Our emotional symptoms are precious sources of life and individuality. —Sir Thomas More

Walter Kirn is a novelist who spends his days mostly alone, imagining the complicated emotional lives of the fictional people he dreams up. But he knows the real world of work as well, since to pay the rent he has always held day jobs as a journalist and book critic. Around the turn of the twenty-first century, he was living in Montana, sharing custody of his two children with his ex-wife, and earning $75,000 a year as a contributor to *Time.* Sweet gig? Sure. But for months, he says, in his conversations with editors he sensed a growing "atmosphere of peril. I mean, you couldn't turn on the TV without seeing something on the AOL/Time Warner merger that was the cock of the century."

Walter's first big-time occupational emotion: *anxiety.*

Late one afternoon in 2003, he was in Minnesota, where he'd grown up, visiting his mother. He'd just taken his 3-year-old son and 6-year-old daughter to their first professional baseball game in Minneapolis and was sitting in the parking lot of the stadium on a sweltering-hot day. Of course, because the universe was *completely* malfunctioning, the air conditioner in his car had also just quit. Then his editor called.

Few of us have the ability to maintain any measure of professional distance or objectivity when little kids are clamoring in the background, but for Walter to try to do so in that context—hyperexcited-on-the-brink-of-collapse kids in a broiling car—well, the timing for a call from his editor couldn't have been worse. "The corporate jargon was so silky," he said, "at first I wasn't sure whether I was being presented a noose or a velvet necktie, the way he put it. 'Your job has been "*rethought,*" and now you're going to have the opportunity to make even more money if you pitch a story and we accept it.' "

Rethought? Really? Walter was being fired, plain and simple. Sure it was a demotion to freelancer with sugarcoated "opportunities," but the reality was no more regular paychecks and no benefits. Given his general state of anticipatory anxiety, "it wasn't a total surprise," he said, "but the smoothness and the indirectness of it felt a little patronizing—and infuriating on a deep level. I would have much preferred a cleaner cut. I had to sort through the corporate-speak, so my emotions were delayed."

Walter's second big-time occupational emotion: *anger.*

His first thought after he hung up the phone was, " 'Oh, *shit.*' I was in front of my kids in the car, so I couldn't cry. And then I was in front of my mother, and couldn't cry in front of her, either." Adding insult to injury, Walter ended up in his childhood room, crying. "It was kind of motionless crying, where tears just came down my cheeks."

Walter's standard by-product of occupational emotion: *crying.*

Walter didn't have a cathartic, wobbly kind of breakdown, but rather had a feeling of the bottom having been slid artfully out from under his feet. "I was divorced," he said, "and in a very precarious financial position where just a few checks were keeping it all afloat, and now they were gone." In other words, Walter now shared the emotional precipice that the downsized, laid-off, and fired feel when faced with the rock-and-hard-place exigencies of real life.

Walter's third big-time occupational emotion: *fear.*

Now consider another emotionally fraught scene. It's in a standard-issue American corporate office. Three people are present. Behind an office desk sit Ryan, a smiling, confident, 45-year-old gray-haired man and Natalie, 23, a nervous but alert young woman, both in crisp dark suits. Sitting across from them is a balding 55-year-old man—we'll call him Steve—wearing a sleeves-rolled-up plaid shirt, necktie, and chinos. Ryan and Natalie lean forward; the older man leans back. Everyone is anxious, but the older man's anxiety is turning to anger and fear, because these two young strangers are informing him that he's being laid off.

Does the scene sound familiar? It should if you've seen the Oscar-nominated movie *Up in the Air*—which happens to be an adaptation of a novel written by Walter Kirn two years before *Time* fired him. Walter's fictional 45-year-old, played in the film by George Clooney, is Ryan Bingham, a professional labor force "hit man" who travels the country firing people for a company called Career Transition Counseling. As Clooney introduces his character at the beginning of the film: "I work for another company that lends me out to pussies like Steve's boss, who don't have the balls to sack their own employees." Think about the choice of words Clooney uses to describe his work: "pussies," "balls," "sack." They are aggressive, emasculating words suggestive of powerful emotional states: pride, arrogance, and pity on his part; fear and cowardice on the part of the executives who hire him; and fear, anxiety, and humiliation on the part of poor losers who will be fired.

Clooney is the postmodern terminator, descending from 30,000 feet 322 days a year into one office or another, delivering his rehearsed script, in particular the disingenuous and cynical line, "Anyone who's ever built an empire or changed the world has sat where you're sitting now . . ." giving the illusion of caring without actually engaging, leaving behind shocked wrecks as he glides out the door. It is an art that he's perfected and that he's even turned into a public-speaking shtick about living without emotional attachment to anything.

When Natalie, played by Anna Kendrick, is hired by Career Transition Counseling to implement the ultimate in emotion-free downsizing—termination by live Internet video—Clooney is forced by his boss to take her on the road to ensure that her beta program incorporates all of Clooney's expertise into its launch.

We watch Clooney's character, the epitome of emotional detachment, the *"Imagine waking up tomorrow with nothing. It's kinda exhilarating, isn't it?"* motivational speaker, deny and grapple with anger and fear at losing his own job as a result of Natalie's innovation. The emptiness of his life looms as he contemplates his own unemployment. And we watch Kendrick's growing recognition, prodded by Clooney's seasoned (ersatz) empathy, that her virtual termination system robs people of dignity, as, finally, she's galvanized to quit after one of her terminees commits suicide. Rarely has the messy, human emotional undertow of work life been so artfully captured.

THE HISTORY OF EMOTION

While there have been other memorable artistic explorations of how emotion drives our workplace behavior—Cary Grant and Rosalind Russell's 1940 *His Girl Friday,* Faye Dunaway and William Holden's 1976 *Network,* Michael Douglas's 1987 *Wall Street,* Albert Brooks and Holly Hunter's 1987 *Broadcast News,* and Sigourney Weaver and Melanie Griffith's 1988 *Working Girl,* to name a few—the scientific study of emotion began in 1872, with the publication of Charles Darwin's *The Expression of Emotions in Man and Animals.* A dozen years after he had revolutionized the understanding of biology and human existence with *Origin of the Species,* Darwin analyzed minute human facial expressions and determined that each signaled a specific emotion, consistent across genders and cultures. He observed that each of us expresses certain emotions like fear or surprise in precisely the same ways through tiny nonverbal facial cues—the raised eyebrow registering surprise, the downturned mouth registering disgust, and so on. Darwin classified six primary or universal emotions—happiness, sadness, fear, anger, surprise, and disgust—each of which, we now know, is the result of a complex sequence of neural responses. Harvard psychologist William James launched the psychological study of emotion in 1884 in the journal *Mind* with the publication of his essay "What Is an Emotion?" in which he explored the origins of emotion.

From the time of the earliest humans, recognizing fear on a comrade's face triggered an impulse to act—to flee, escaping the shared danger, or to help him fight, collaboratively overcoming the threat. Expressions of happiness encouraged familial or community bonding. Darwin and James understood that our emotions, far from being irrational or unimportant, are universal tools that help us read cues that allow us to successfully navigate our environment. They established, in other words, the oft-forgotten notion that emotional fluency can mean the difference between survival and death, or success and failure, and that it therefore figures importantly in evolution. Our nervous system allows us to calculate and synthesize all the complex environmental cues (visual, aural, olfactory, social), processing instant judgments derived from universal physical signifiers as well as emotional "dialects" specific to race, gender, social class, and occupation, among others. One could argue that from customer service reps to teachers to nurses to managers, this ability to "read" emotions is a skill that remains as essential to professional success as it was to our ancient ancestors' physical survival.

Getting clear about which kinds of emotions became workplace-approved also requires a brief recapitulation of the millennia-long tension—a struggle? a dance? maybe a tango?—between reason and emotion as a governing principle in society.

The familiar cartoon of a person with a mischievous red devil (emotion, evil, id) whispering in one ear while a white-clad angel (reason, good, superego) whispers in the other comes to mind. This conceit was perhaps inspired in part by a metaphor Plato created more than 2,300 years ago to explain the perpetual conflict between emotion and reason. In *Phaedrus,* Plato presents a portrait of the battle our souls endure between reason, depicted as a white horse, "upright and clean-limbed," and passion, a very different kind of horse, "with thick short neck, black skin . . . hot-blooded, consorting with wantonness and vainglory . . . hard to control." Bad things were done *to* us by our emotions. We made good things happen *for* us through the discipline of reason.

During the seventeenth century, René "I think, therefore I am" Descartes, the mathematician and philosopher, imposed a mathematical rigor on the exploration of human knowledge and emphatically reargued the case for reason being the ultimate, refined tool that people have for properly shaping the world. With the industrial revolution the factory became the paradigmatic workplace, and ever-larger factories became a manifestation of modern hyperrationality. Divisions of labor, interchangeable parts, organizational charts, and timetables made factories—and then offices—into temples of strict rationalism.

But it is merely a *presumed* rationality, a frequently fake, superficial ultrarationality. As management scholar Blake Ashforth wrote in *Emotions in the Workplace,* "Organizational practitioners and scholars often maintain the convenient fiction that organizations are cool arenas for dispassionate thought and action. Hierarchies, job descriptions, budgets, policies, operating procedures, training regimens, reward systems, and so on are implicitly thought to legislate against intrusive and unseemly emotions."

Neuroscientists are now discovering that the opposite is closer to the truth. By mapping our brains' neural circuitry through the emerging technology of functional magnetic resonance imaging, researchers today have direct, detailed access to *living* human brains, identifying in what part of the brain what kind of emotional response is occurring, triggered by and in turn triggering what kind of reaction—thus demonstrating in deep, empirical ways that emotion is essential in all aspects of our lives.

With the publication of *Descartes' Error: Emotion, Reason and the Human Brain,* neuroscientist Antonio Damásio, now the head of the University of Southern California's Brain and Creativity Institute, rocked his academic worlds by showing that emotions were as essential to rational behavior as strictly cognitive brain function. Indeed, studies by Damásio and others have demonstrated that *without* the tempering commonsense effects of emotions, it is literally impossible to make everyday decisions.

Hanna Damásio, a professor of psychology and neurology at USC and Antonio's wife, led one of the first efforts to demonstrate this. She and her team of fellow researchers re-created the virtual brain of Phineas Gage, a nineteenth-century railroad construction worker who had a foot-long iron spike accidentally driven through his skull. Gage survived, but the injury destroyed his orbito-frontal cortex—which has now been identified as integral to emotion control—and completely altered his personality. He went from being a mild-mannered, responsible employee to a seemingly irrational man driven by his passions. A contemporary assessment of his brain made the rough causal connection between severe damage to his orbito-frontal cortex and his loss of social inhibition, but until Hanna Damásio's computer-generated cerebral model, it had all been speculative. As Antonio Damásio writes in *Descartes' Error,* "Hanna and her colleagues could say with some foundation that it was selective damage in the prefrontal cortices of Phineas Gage's brain that compromised his ability to plan for the future, to conduct himself according to the social rules he previously had learned, and to decide on the course of action that ultimately would be most advantageous to his survival."

Descartes notwithstanding, we are learning that it might be at least as accurate to say *I feel, therefore I am.*

SO WHAT IS EMOTION?

At its most basic, an emotion is a hardwired *biological* component of our physiology, and emotions are as essential to survival as other automatic, purely physical regulatory processes such as metabolism and muscular reflex responses. We do not get angry and *then* have our blood pressure rise—rather, our blood pressure rises in *response* to some stimulus, which causes our bodies to experience what we have learned to label *anger.* What we call emotion is simply how we mediate between environmental stimuli and subsequent behavior, and the labels by which we mentally index those stimuli and behaviors for later reference.

On the most elementary level, at the first whiff of danger the amygdala, seated underneath the neocortex and one of the most primitive parts of our brains, triggers the release of the stress hormones—adrenaline and cortisol among others—that have the effect of raising our blood pressure, sending more blood to our muscles, thereby making us more alert in preparation to fight or flee the imminent threat. Additionally, the release of stress hormones allows us to encode an emotional memory more effectively, reminding us that what we are feeling is important to remember another time. This is why emotional memories are associated with stronger subjective feelings and are more easily recalled. Whether I'm cowering from an angry boss, stopping my kid from running in front of a speeding car, or watching a scary movie, the amgydala responds, on a basic level, in a very similar way.

But while the amygdala's response to each of those different experiences is the same—causing my brain to register fear as the emotion felt—the resolution for each kind of fear is different. Stopping my kid from running into oncoming traffic is an example of a real danger averted, similar to what our ancestors experienced when escaping a predator. The hormones released by my body are expended, leaving me tired but calm. Similarly, a skillful filmmaker will capitalize on the imaginary fear he incites to make me jump, gasp, or laugh as the movie unreels, those physical reactions again allowing my body to dissipate some of the artificially induced but nonetheless very real stress hormones motivated by this fear response. It is only with my fear of the boss, where the lack of an appropriate *physical* response causes the adrenaline and cortisol to linger in my body—an unsatisfactory resolution that causes me to end up in an extended, free-floating anxiety state that leaves me agitated and disturbed—that I become unnecessarily distressed. Emotion is far more complicated in a modern work setting than it was for our ancestors on the savanna. On the job, as I've said, we're dealing mainly in the psychological realm, where perceived assaults on our egos, our social standing, or our value to the community are far more subjective in the ways they put us at risk.

This is the crux of the issue for us modern people: our *Homo sapiens* bodies, pretty much as they did 200,000 years ago, continue to *automatically* process psychological threats as physical threats. Deep inside we are all irredeemably *very* old school. But the reality is that reacting to a psychological threat with a physical response is wildly inappropriate. And this disconnect—the evolutionary lag in the development of more emotionally calibrated or sophisticated responses to psychological challenges—is a huge contributor to what makes navigating modern life so incredibly hard. Whether we're watching *Nightmare on Elm Street 27* or dealing with a duplicitous coworker, our bodies tell us to do one thing, while our minds know that we cannot or should not. Two of the behaviors that ensured our species' survival—fighting and fleeing—would be, on the job, inappropriate, shocking, and grounds for dismissal. Imagine a sales assistant leaping over the counter to pummel a nasty customer, or flouncing off the floor, running away from the unpleasant encounter. Yet our bodies persist in wanting us to do exactly as we have done for eons. It's this ancient-versus-modern struggle that lurks behind much of the current crisis of emotion in the workplace. Terry Burnham, the author of *Mean Markets and Lizard Brains: How to Profit From the New Science of Irrationality,* is an economist who puts it this way: "The caricature view would be, the caveman wins the battle, has more babies, crushes his enemies, then puts on a suit 10,000 years later and goes into a boardroom and still wants to crush his enemies."

To further complicate the picture, in the larger culture we harbor paradoxical notions about the value of expressing our feelings—bottling up our emotions is bad for us, but letting them out also can make things worse. To say that the messages are mixed is an understatement. And how is a person to behave when angry or upset at work, where keeping our emotions in check is viewed as integral to success? If you factor in the range of individual, biologically determined emotional wiring—my sensitive nature versus Cyndi's laissez-faire one—figuring out what's considered acceptable emotional expressiveness becomes even more confusing.

This contradiction between what was evolutionarily essential for our survival and what is appropriate and effective in the contemporary workplace is what makes a usable guide to optimizing emotion at work so challenging. Simply put, we are still (very slowly) evolving, needing to learn new behavioral patterns before our brains and nervous systems have caught up with modern, mostly physical-predator-free lives.

THE GENDER FACTOR

Today we know that women and men's brains are, in some important ways, structurally and biochemically different, and that therefore how the genders experience and regulate emotion tends to be different. For instance, the hippocampus, a significant memory center in the brain, and the neural pathways connected to other parts of the brain responsible for language and observing emotions are *physically larger* in women. As a result, apparently, women are on average better at remembering and articulating the details of an emotional event. Not only might a woman in a workplace, for instance, remember what every member of a negotiating team was wearing on a given day, she may also be able to describe in minute detail each interaction, how each person made her feel, and in turn how she made the others feel. Dr. Louann Brizendine, the founder of the Women's Mood and Hormone Clinic at the University of California, San Francisco, believes that "the female brain is so deeply affected by hormones that their influence can be said to create a woman's reality. . . . [W]omen have an eight-lane superhighway for processing emotion, while men have a small country road."

Women also produce higher levels of prolactin, the hormone that controls tears, which means that generally women are, in fact, hardwired to cry more frequently. So, yes, women do cry more than men, but it's not because we're weaker or less rational;

it's how we're built. (In Chapter Seven, I talk a lot more about crying.)

When under stress, both men and women release cortisol and epinephrine, the hormones that raise a person's blood pressure, increase their blood sugar levels, and control their "fight-or-flight" response. But women under stress also produce significantly more oxytocin, the hormone that influences what biologists call the "tend and befriend" instinct. "From a neurobiological point of view," Daniel Goleman says, "we know that women's brains are more replete with oxytocin, the hormone that encourages social bonding, and the more social people are, the more socially intelligent they tend to be."

A man's brain, on the other hand, has larger centers for action and aggression than a woman's does, and while both men and women produce testosterone, men produce ten times more than women. A man would therefore be far more likely to confront the interrupting jerk in the meeting—to fight the aggressor. Because of the way the male brain is wired, a public confrontation with an interrupter might ultimately give a man a positive adrenaline boost. Additionally, because a competitive environment stimulates the production of testosterone, a feedback loop can propel men toward even riskier behavior. On the other hand, in women, Brizendine writes, "conflict is more likely to set in motion a cascade of negative chemical reactions, creating feelings of stress, upset, and fear." In other words, after the fact, for *biological* reasons, women regret expressing anger more than men do.

When under stress a man's field of vision narrows, allowing him to zero in, visually eliminating every extraneous detail outside of the threat, undoubtedly a useful trick for our ancestral hunters, while for women, the opposite tends to happen. In a 2006 paper, "Why Sex Matters for Neuroscience," published in *Nature Reviews Neuroscience,* Larry Cahill reported that "in both rats and monkeys, chronic stress causes damage to the hippocampus in males, but does so far less, if at all in females." Under stress a woman's field of vision widens, allowing her to take in her total surroundings—a trait selected for by evolution, perhaps, to better detect threats to her children. If you ever wondered how your third-grade teacher Miss Ross or your colleague Amy called you out when you were off to the side of the room mimicking their gestures during presentations, now you know.

In their 2008 paper on gender differences, five psychologists—Kateri McRae and James Gross of Stanford, Kevin Ochsner of Columbia, Iris Mauss of the University of Denver, and John Gabrieli of MIT—reported that while men and women don't really differ in their "reactivity," or the number of milliseconds it takes to react to some emotional provocation, they are quite different in the ways in which they later manage their emotional reactions.

Based on both self-report and neural responses to aversive photos as measured by fMRI brain scans, the authors discovered no significant differences between the genders in the speed of their reactions to stimuli. But on closer examination of the data, the scientists discovered significant gender distinctions in how men and women were able to *regulate* their emotional response to these stimuli. The amygdala was less activated in men's brains than in women's, and portions of the women's prefrontal cortex, the cognitive control center, were more active than were those of the men. The increased number of prefrontral regions of the brain that women used to regulate their emotions suggested to the authors that women may have to use more effort to attempt to control emotions. Additionally, women showed higher activity in a region in the brain associated with reward processing than men, suggesting that as a way to regulate their behavior women may attempt to transform negative emotions into more positive experiences.

If you always wondered why men told jokes in the hallway after a tough meeting, it turns out that they may really have a *biologically* easier time dealing with difficult emotional situations. The metaphorical water does run off their backs. This is good to know. It helps to demystify that folk sense that women chew over problems more and recognize that the tendency is not a fault but simply how women are wired. Knowing that women's natural neurological approach to regulating their emotions is more effortful and entails trying to shift them into something more positive is also helpful in suggesting strategies for women trying to build up their emotional resiliency.

Without the benefit of this kind of scientific insight into our neurobiological processes it's easy to see why from an early age and in spite of the acute modern sensitivity to anything smacking of gender bias, biologically informed gender behaviors lead to pervasive cultural stereotyping that in turn reinforces those very gender differences.

Where girls play house or school, boys play war and other games of aggression. At toy stores, girls are sold dolls and arts and crafts, boys action figures, building sets, and gadgets. For boys it's cool to scream and yell and charge up a hill, with "boys will be boys" justifying the behavior. Little boys play at being heroes and learn strategies that employ history, team building, and problem solving. Little girls are encouraged to engage in nurturing play, starting out with baby dolls to simulate mothering and graduating to dolls that reinforce an interest in beauty, fashion, and general princessy-ness. And princesses? They do not *work* to achieve their status, and (outside of *King Lear*) they don't get angry. From toddlerhood on, girls are taught to collaborate, to be empathetic, and to be "nice" above all—reinforcing gender norms and strengthening those gender-based kinds of neural connections. In fact, researchers now know that early experience, in what neuroscientists call *shaping plasticity,* actually affects the growth, function, and chemistry of the genes inside our cells. While it used to be commonplace to believe that our temperaments were developed through the dominance of either nature *or* nurture, it is, in fact, becoming clear that we grow via a constant interplay between the two. What we experience (nurture) influences our neurobiological (nature) development *and* our neurobiology, in turn, determines how we react to our environment. As Lise Eliot, an associate professor of neuroscience at the Chicago Medical School wrote in *Scientific American Mind,* "Genes and hormones light the spark for most boy-girl differences, but the flame is strongly fanned by the essentially separate cultures in which boys and girls grow up. Appreciating *how* sex differences emerge can reduce dangerous stereotyping and give parents and teachers ideas for cross-training boys' and girls' minds, to minimize their more troubling discrepancies and enable all children to more fully develop their diverse talents."

These gender-based differences—in some cases biologically based, in all cases culturally reinforced—reverberate in different ways within our society, and those reverberations have major relevance at work. In her provocative book, *You Just Don't Understand: Women and Men in Conversation,* the pioneering Georgetown University linguistics professor Deborah Tannen deconstructed the significantly different ways in which men and women talk to one another, and concluded that we are acculturated in ways that result in women seeking to "connect" open-endedly to others in conversation, whereas men are far more "transactional"—you-do-this-for-me, I'll-do-this-for-you—in their exchanges. As a result of these different communication styles, Tannen suggests, women tend to feel unheard by men.

The title of John Gray's bestseller *Men Are from Mars, Women Are from Venus* quickly became *the* catchphrase distilling the idea that women and men are radically different in their emotional styles and modes of communication. When that book came out almost two decades ago, the neuroscience was sketchy, and the belief at the time was that any mental or behavioral differences between the sexes were entirely products of the male-dominated culture. Now, as academic researchers are finding, the ways in which the genders behave is a far more nuanced interplay between nature and nurture.

EMOTIONAL INTELLIGENCE

The belief that an awareness of emotions, one's own and others, is as central to maximizing worldly success as IQ has gained real traction over the past twenty years. In the 1990s, Daniel Goleman identified four main components of emotional competency in *Emotional Intelligence*—self-awareness (perceiving), self-management (using), social awareness (understanding), and relationship management (managing)—and applied these traits to the workplace, presenting case study after case study showing how organizations that operate in emotionally intelligent ways can be more competitive.

Goleman has never isolated women as a focus for study, but he does believe that "there are ways that women are emotionally intelligent at work that men are not. Research derived from the ESCI tool"—his diagnostic survey designed to help people assess their emotional and social competencies within organizations—"indicates that women tend to be stronger than men on social intelligence skills like making people feel harmonious." Interestingly, though, Goleman also pointed me to studies showing that "women are also more sophisticated in emotional *aggression*. When girls are younger, there is not such a distinction, but at puberty, when boys continue to be more aggressively physically expressive, girls become more *emotionally* aggressive." By this

Goleman doesn't mean that girls become screaming tyrants, but rather that as most boys mature into a degree of physical superiority, and because physical aggression is more taboo for girls, girls learn to read and express, perhaps protectively, a more finely calibrated range of emotional nuance.

Goleman is also careful to note that while women tend in some ways to become more emotionally expressive and fluent than men, the difference is not so absolute as to exclude high emotional intelligence among men as well. Just as some women do indeed succeed at the highest levels of science and engineering, so are some men emotional virtuosos. Jeffrey Sonnenfeld, the Senior Associate Dean for Executive Programs at the Yale School of Management, says that "it is important not to presume emotional intelligence for [all] women. There are some women, like [the California Republican Senate nominee and former Hewlett-Packard CEO] Carly Fiorina, who are far tougher and meaner than many men." Both Goleman and Sonnenfeld seem to suggest that we may be approaching a time when rigid perceptions regarding "appropriate" gender behavior—that tough women are anomalous, somehow less true to their inherent feminine nature or that men lack emotional intelligence—may be softening to encompass the notion that a full spectrum of emotional expression can be found within each gender.

And while there is a growing consensus among the scientific and academic communities that the ways in which women and men produce different kinds and amounts of hormones tend, on balance, to make the genders quite different as emotional beings—who respond differently to differing emotional stressors—what has yet to emerge is an understanding of how this will influence organizational behaviors and norms, and how those new norms will influence our collective wiring. Examining this reciprocity is another objective of *It's Always Personal.*

A NEW NATIONAL PORTRAIT OF EMOTION AT WORK

As I explored the cultural and scientific issues surrounding emotion in the workplace, I began to worry that I might have put on self-justifying blinders, convincing myself that emotional exchanges in the workplace were more common, confusing, and relevant to people than they actually are. To a hammer, the proverb says, everything is a nail to pound. Perhaps I had overhyped the repercussions associated with crying or shouting at work because of my own history with them. Before climbing further down into my own echo chamber, I decided that I needed to get a good, detailed portrait of the whole phenomenon in some statistically valid way.

Delving deeper into the literature to see if relevant, real-world national research and data existed, I discovered that while there are myriad studies looking at emotion, nearly all were conducted by psychologists or neurobiologists in controlled laboratory experiments, trying to isolate single catalysts for anger, fear, or anxiety. Conversely, there are broad, anecdotal digests that present loosely strung together after-the-fact interviews compiled by consultants or social scientists that focused primarily on the skills that might help people, in the abstract, to control their inner demons. The academic studies are limited, dry, and rather far removed from the multidimensional complexity of real-life experience. And the social-scientific studies tend to lack breadth and useful depth. There was absolutely nothing I could find that answered the basic question: how comfortable are Americans with emotions at work?

It occurred to me that one logical place to turn for help would be an advertising agency. After all, these agencies are in the business of microscopically dissecting consumer preferences and then aggregating those results into statistically valid and useful patterns, and that felt very similar to what I was hoping to do with people's real-life experiences of emotions at work.

I also knew that the kind of research I was interested in would require a substantial commitment of resources, both human and financial. The only way I could imagine getting any organization to play along would be if it had a paying client for whom emotion was relevant. And then I remembered the "Let It Out" campaign for Kleenex tissues. I went to the Kleenex website and right at the top of the home page was the statement "It feels good to feel." Within the "Experience the Release" portion of the site there was an entire section devoted to letting people log in to share crying experiences. I had no doubt that if Kleenex would have me, it could be an ideal partner. I discovered that J. Walter Thompson (JWT) is the agency that handles the Kleenex account and, much to my surprise, Rosemarie Ryan, at the time the president of JWT North America, agreed to meet. Over the course of an hour we had a free-ranging conversation about the changing nature of the workplace—its general "loosening," its feminization, and more—and the sense that a freedom to bring more of our authentic selves to work could be a valuable twenty-first-century goal. If JWT's research department could shed real light on what was really going on with emotion in the workplace right now, it agreed to be in.

If much of what this book is about is people behaving badly, with their emotions out of control, my experience with the team at JWT has been precisely the opposite. While it may sound like sycophancy, the truth is that the agency put its money and its spirit behind a project that offered it no immediate financial upside—and did so during the Great Recession to boot. The experience has restored a bit of my faith in corporate America's ability to envision research and development in innovative ways. JWT took a huge risk with me, and for that I will be forever grateful.

But enough fawning. What did we find out?

In the spring of 2009 Mark Truss, JWT's director of brand intelligence, and I fielded the first of our two national polls, the Emotional Incidents in the Workplace Survey, targeting men and women between 18 and 64. We surveyed 701 respondents, a random sample representing every state and the full range of occupational levels and business sectors, equally divided by gender.

We were interested in getting a snapshot of what kinds of emotions are most prevalent in contemporary work environments. We asked a total of ninety questions exploring an individual's perception of emotion—ranging from happiness to hopelessness—over a period of time. For instance, what did a respondent feel before, during, and after crying, getting angry, or feeling despondent? Were those emotions related to his or her work or not? We also sought to get a sense of how a respondent felt about others when they expressed certain emotions at work. I've included a few of the questions below. If you'd like to see the full survey, please visit AnneKreamer.com.

Thinking about the past 12 months, which, if any, of the following feelings have you experienced while at work? (Select as many as apply.)

- ❍ Happiness
- ❍ Anger
- ❍ Frustration
- ❍ A sense of accomplishment
- ❍ Annoyance
- ❍ Pride
- ❍ Uncertainty
- ❍ Hopelessness
- ❍ Felt like crying
- ❍ Anxiety
- ❍ Fear
- ❍ None of the above

In the past 12 months, have you cried while you were at work, for any reason? By "for any reason" we mean that it could have been related to work or not related to work, and it could be because of something that you experienced or because of something that someone else experienced that affected you. (Select one.)

- ❍ Yes
- ❍ No

For the next series of questions, please think about the last time you cried at work in the past 12 months. Which of the following circumstances were affecting you the last time you cried at work? (Select all that apply.)

- ❍ A negative performance review
- ❍ Feeling bullied by a colleague
- ❍ A run-in with a colleague you dislike/are competitive with/are threatened by
- ❍ Others in your workplace not doing what they were supposed to do
- ❍ A rude customer/client
- ❍ Someone yelling/snapping at you
- ❍ Not being given appropriate resources, materials, or time to execute a job requirement
- ❍ Someone taking credit for your accomplishment
- ❍ Change of your responsibilities/duties
- ❍ Being laid off
- ❍ A colleague being laid off
- ❍ Being unfairly blamed or criticized for something
- ❍ Your accomplishment not being acknowledged or recognized
- ❍ Anxiety over layoffs/downsizing

- ❍ Stress from home spilling over into work
- ❍ Sick child, significant other, parent, sibling, or other relative
- ❍ Your health
- ❍ Getting/having your period or a "hormonal moment"
- ❍ Someone you work with experiencing a death in the family or other family crisis
- ❍ Someone you work with experiencing something positive
- ❍ Someone you work with being unfairly blamed or criticized for something
- ❍ Being overwhelmed (crying was your way of coping)
- ❍ Other (specify) __________

Still thinking about the last time you cried at work, which of the following words best describes the way you felt the moment before you cried? (Select one.)

- ❍ Angry
- ❍ Happy
- ❍ Embarrassed
- ❍ Self-healing
- ❍ Frustrated
- ❍ Annoyed
- ❍ Humiliated
- ❍ Uncertain
- ❍ Hopeless
- ❍ Relieved
- ❍ Unprofessional
- ❍ Relaxed
- ❍ Out-of-control
- ❍ Inferior
- ❍ Satisfied
- ❍ Awkward
- ❍ Confused

- ❍ In control
- ❍ Overwhelmed
- ❍ Sad
- ❍ Weak
- ❍ Strong
- ❍ Honest
- ❍ Vulnerable
- ❍ None of the above

While you were crying, how did you feel? (Select one.)

- ❍ Angry
- ❍ Happy
- ❍ Embarrassed
- ❍ Self-healing
- ❍ Frustrated
- ❍ Annoyed
- ❍ Humiliated
- ❍ Uncertain
- ❍ Hopeless
- ❍ Relieved
- ❍ Unprofessional
- ❍ Relaxed
- ❍ Out-of-control
- ❍ Inferior
- ❍ Satisfied
- ❍ Awkward
- ❍ Confused
- ❍ In control
- ❍ Overwhelmed
- ❍ Sad
- ❍ Weak

- ❍ Strong
- ❍ Honest
- ❍ Vulnerable
- ❍ None of the above

After the incident was over, how did you feel? (Select one.)

- ❍ Angry
- ❍ Happy
- ❍ Embarrassed
- ❍ Self-healing
- ❍ Frustrated
- ❍ Annoyed
- ❍ Humiliated
- ❍ Uncertain
- ❍ Hopeless
- ❍ Relieved
- ❍ Unprofessional
- ❍ Relaxed
- ❍ Out-of-control
- ❍ Inferior
- ❍ Satisfied
- ❍ Awkward
- ❍ Confused
- ❍ In control
- ❍ Overwhelmed
- ❍ Sad
- ❍ Weak
- ❍ Strong
- ❍ Honest
- ❍ Vulnerable
- ❍ None of the above

In what way(s) do you think people viewed you differently because you cried at work? (Select as many as apply.)

I think they viewed me as . . .

- ❍ Weak
- ❍ Unstable
- ❍ Unprofessional
- ❍ Childish
- ❍ Overly emotional
- ❍ Not management material
- ❍ Girly
- ❍ Brave
- ❍ Not afraid to express myself
- ❍ Whiny
- ❍ Manipulative
- ❍ Unable to handle stress
- ❍ Passionate
- ❍ Caring
- ❍ Vulnerable
- ❍ Other (specify) ________

Here are our most important findings:

- *Frustration* is the dominant emotion Americans say they feel at work, with nearly three in four (73 percent) saying they've felt frustrated.
- Women say they feel *anger* at work slightly more than men say they do (44 percent of women versus 38 percent of men), though it's a primary feeling among the younger (ages 18–44) women, 51 percent of whom report feeling angry, compared to only 42 percent of men in the same age group.

- Many young men (42 percent), however, feel that anger is an effective management tool, versus only 23 percent of young women.
- More than 60 percent of all workers reported that they saw their boss get angry with someone during the past year.
- Nearly half (46 percent) of workers recall feeling *anxiety* in the past year, with only slightly higher (49 percent) numbers for women than for men (43 percent). Young women feel the most anxious (56 percent), especially when compared with young men (38 percent).
- Not surprisingly, we found the largest differential in emotional expressiveness to be the gap between younger women and older men, but the scale of that difference is striking: *women under 45 are ten times more likely to cry at work* than men 45 and older.
- And women do indeed cry much more than men. During just the previous 12 months, 41 percent of women cried at work, but only 9 percent of men.
- In some ways, women and men are not all that different—both genders reported that anger, frustration, annoyance, and anxiety had made them cry at work.
- Surprisingly, whether or not someone had cried at work seems to make *no difference* in how much they like their job, for either men or women.

That's right: while one might assume that a person who cries is chronically unhappy at work, that's not what our respondents reported. And we also discovered that there is no "crying ceiling"—successful people from every level of the professional hierarchy reported that they cried at work, bosses as well as junior staff. While the data shows that younger people and women cry more frequently than older people and men, discovering that people at all *levels* of employment cried—and admitted it—

surprised me. Now let me repeat this: *people who sometimes cry at work are not necessarily unhappy in their jobs,* and people who sometimes cry at work are also able to *ascend high within the management ranks.*

Also significant were findings that indicate that workers don't find emotion in the workplace to necessarily be a bad thing:

- Most people (69 percent) feel that when someone gets emotional in the workplace it makes the person seem more human.
- And finally, a whopping 88 percent of all workers (93 percent women and 83 percent men) feel that being sensitive to others' emotions at work is an asset, a positive trait.

So while I was happy to be confirmed in my basic hypothesis that Americans across the board feel bombarded by emotions on the job, I was frankly surprised by what I saw as the counterintuitively high percentage of those who see emotion at work as potentially *positive and humanizing.* This finding really flew in the face of the prevalent notion that showing a lot of emotion at work is a bad thing. It also underscored for me that the moment is ripe to seriously reevaluate how we can *use* emotion more effectively on the job.

Using emotion to our advantage entails developing a portfolio of skills to deal with a variety of circumstances. Throughout the rest of the book, under the heading of EMT (Emotional Management Toolkit) I offer a variety of different strategies—from expert opinion, to step-by-step guides, to personal reflections—for dealing with a range of emotionally charged workplace challenges. Pick and choose among the suggestions those that work best for you, and build an individually tailored emotion management portfolio. What is important is that each approach you choose feels natural and as if it will be helpful when you're dealing with a difficult emotional situation.

Now let's examine the main kinds of emotions people discussed feeling most powerfully on the job—anger, fear, anxiety, and joy. We'll also explore in greater detail the subject of tears, which are associated with all of these emotions, as well as empathy, which is our ability to understand or feel the emotional or mental state of another.

THREE

The Anger Epidemic

Anyone can become angry—that is easy. But to become angry with the right person, to the right degree, at the right time, for the right purpose, and in the right way—that is not easy. —Aristotle

THE GOOD, THE BAD, AND THE ANGRY

Before Jim Cramer created his CNBC program *Mad Money,* he ran a very successful several-hundred-million-dollar hedge fund, where he was, by his own admission, notorious for violent rages. But he also credits his free-flowing anger with much of his success.

"I was so angry all the time. I used my anger as fuel to make money. Right up front I had the good sense to say to people [I hired] that this is going to be a horrible experience," that they had to "stick with a crazy person and make a bargain with the devil and be willing to subject yourself to humiliation. And I will promise you, you will be rich if you stay with me. And everybody did. There wasn't anybody who worked for me who didn't get rich, and after they got rich I *expected* them to come in and say, 'I hate you! Fuck you, Jim!' "

By financial-industry standards Jim's behavior wasn't even so extreme. Wall Street is a culture that thrives on risky behavior, a pedal-to-the-metal, take-it-on-the-chin kind of macho bravado. And in Jim's case, the anger drove profits: between 1987, when he started, and 2001, when he left, his hedge fund was performing among the top five, appreciating at an annual compound rate of 24 percent, versus a rise in the Dow Average of less than 11 percent.

Even as Jim delivered impressive returns for his investors, his anger came at a tremendous emotional price for his employees—in spite of giving fair warning about his behavior to impending hires. "Men [who worked for me] cried because I was so vile. I was ill. I remember that I made people cry [deliberately], so that they remembered so much pain [that] they'd never screw up again. I made people wear shirts inside out and had them walk outside—anything for pure humiliation, so that they wouldn't make the same mistake again." Jim's behavior became so out of whack that he once sent a guy home and "told him to go be with his mother and gave him a note to give her saying he'd been a bad boy and that I'd fired him."

THE MESSAGE IS THE MEDIUM

While most of us will never deal with someone as vituperative as Jim was during that phase of his life, it's no surprise that Donald Trump, another emotionally demonstrative person, understood that Jim's *extreme* emotional expressiveness would translate particularly well from the real world to the make-believe of TV, and invited him to be a guest judge during the seventh season of *The Apprentice.* Whether it's CBS's *Big Brother* and *Survivor,* MTV's *Real World,* NBC's *The Biggest Loser,* or even Fox's *American Idol,* the ability to incite a passionate response in the home viewer is how a contestant and/or show becomes successful. Excessive displays of emotion are now a means of competitive differentiation. The modern entertainment-industrial complex enables and encourages *bogus* anger and emotional confrontation among people we don't know and who don't really want to know one another. And as art amplifies reality, the ante for ever-more-thrilling displays of people gone wild is upped and upped and upped.

Thus in popular culture, the mirror through which we see our lives reflected and imagined, it can seem as if America these days is one great hyperbolic seething storm of anger—especially in our current 24/7 cable news-talk radio-blogosphere era. That huge new(ish) maw and the endless cycle of YouTube video replays mean that people-behaving-badly clips rebound perpetually through the culture. Serena Williams's or Roger Federer's unsportsmanlike outbursts are like the tantrums of spoiled children—but instead of averting our eyes and wondering why we, the virtual parents, aren't coolly reprimanding such narcissistic, attention-demanding behavior, our attention is riveted by the famous adults who behave badly, suffer no very serious consequences, and are *rewarded* with talk show pulpits to rationalize their brattiness.

On both sides of the political spectrum, television pundits—from Glenn Beck (who regularly *cries* on the air) to Keith Olbermann (who rants and snorts his way through his annotation of even the day's most pedestrian news)—are no longer dispassionate, fair-minded news-readers but rather performers who act out self-righteous anger and provoke self-righteously angry reactions among their viewers. Those who love each man enjoy their hero's predictably theatrical anger, and enjoy feeling some of it themselves. What's more, if you are partisan toward one, the other is reprehensible, and you can revel in your anger toward him, and toward those who love him. As a result, politicians are now practically obliged to milk trumped-up anger to demonstrate their bona fides as authentic men or women of the people. When Congressman Joe Wilson angrily shouted "You *lie*!" at President Obama during his speech on health care to a joint session of Congress his party elders ritually disapproved, and Wilson confessed afterward that he "let my emotions get the best of me"—although doing so instantly generated $2 million in political contributions. Anger, it seems, pays. But I don't think most of us like this trend, and what can be titillating as a spectator feels disturbing and unpleasant when experienced firsthand.

SO WHAT *IS* ANGER?

As discussed in Chapter Two, anger is one way to interpret the biochemical response to threat by the amygdala. When threatened, we release the hormone epinephrine, followed by norepinephrine (noradrenaline), prepping the body to react—increasing our heart rate and blood pressure, and narrowing our focus as we prepare to fight or flee. But as I also explained, our ability to deal with more subtle and complicated contemporary psychological threats is challenged, since our biological hardware continues to automatically prep us for physical versus verbal responses. Anger in modern life is further complicated because our bodies produce epinephrine not only when we are overstimulated in situations like navigating the stress of workday rush-hour traffic or pitching a deal, but also when we are understimulated or faced with the tedium of dealing with the grinding routine of most jobs. This means that more often than not our jobs prime us for anger.

Workplace anger is often triggered within social situations—an assistant didn't carry his load on a project or the boss didn't acknowledge your efforts—that layer issues of power and status into how safe we feel acknowledging or expressing our anger. That expression can be overtly aggressive or "anger out," as in

Jim Cramer's need to pump himself up to stimulate his competitive edge or eviscerate anyone working for him who delivered less than a full-throttle performance. Or unlike Jim's explosive slash-and-burn blowups, anger over unfair treatment or about a colleague's behavior can linger, unreleased, an "anger in" response leading to more passive kinds of sabotage. In both the passive and aggressive forms of experiencing anger, the behavior tends to become habitual—our "go to" (default) reaction to difficult situations. And over time the more consistently one responds in a certain way, the stronger the underlying neural pathways become, which makes it even more difficult to alter a default response to a situation.

The intensity of our anger is also directly proportional to the degree to which the slight is taken *personally.* If someone told you to get angry right this minute, you'd no doubt fail. But if someone called you a liar or a lazy old fool, it wouldn't take long before you'd feel your anger rising. Interestingly, while researchers have discovered that on average men and women *experience* anger in more or less equal degrees, our biological hardwiring coupled with socially reinforced gender norms leads to very different levels of comfort between the sexes with its *expression.*

> *An angry woman loses status [at work] no matter what her position.*
>
> —Victoria Brescoll, assistant professor, Yale School of Management

On average, it takes greater provocation to make women outwardly express their anger than it does to make men do so, and when they do let it out, they experience greater distress because of the biologically conflicting signals being sent to their brains—one hormone is telling them to snarl, but another wants them to bond. The part of the brain that controls fear, anger, and aggression, the amygdala, is larger in men, predisposing them to express their anger more directly, aggressively, and with greater self-satisfaction. In women, the prefrontal cortex, the *control* center of the brain, is larger, which tends to further encourage nonconfrontational resolutions to conflict. Couple their sense of contradictory physical signals with the culturally reinforced disapproval of angry women and one can see why women feel damned if they don't and *really* damned if they do get angry. A study by psychologist James Averill of the University of Massachusetts of real-world encounters found that while there were no significant differences between men and women in the frequency or causes of angry feelings, women "rated their anger as more intense and out of proportion to the precipitating event than did men."

So in spite of how pervasive displays of anger are in our culture—remember, more than 60 percent of people, according to our survey, are accustomed to seeing anger at work—men and, yes, women remain highly disapproving of angry women on the job.

No woman in the public eye captures our ambivalence about women who show emotion more than Hillary Clinton. In 2006, before Mrs. Clinton decided to run for president, Ken Mehlman, the head of the Republican National Committee, tried to marginalize her chances by declaring that "she seems to have a lot of anger," and "when you think of [her] level of anger, I'm not sure it's what Americans want." As Maureen Dowd responded in *The New York Times,* "They are casting Hillary Clinton as an Angry Woman, a she-monster melding images of Medea, the Furies, harpies . . . This gambit handcuffs Hillary: If she doesn't speak out strongly against President Bush, she's timid and girlie. If she does, she's a witch and a shrew." Any time they're in public, politicians are effectively on the job, so their emotion-at-work displays are perpetually visible and scrutinized. And because Clinton has such strong control over her emotions, whenever they do emerge, they make news. Remember her testy response to the poor Congolese student who innocently asked her to share Bill Clinton's reaction to a trade deal between the Congo and China? "Wait, you want *me* to tell you what my *husband* thinks? My husband is not the secretary of state!"

And that in a nutshell is why women who get angry at work are in a bind. We are expected to be empathetic, caring, nurturing people, and when we don't conform to that not entirely illegitimate stereotype and actually show anger, we risk our professional standing. But on the other hand, we empowered women are expected to be firm, tough, and stalwart—like men—but not a *bitch,* God forbid.

Media management consultant Sandy Kresch knows what it feels like to be caught in that trap. Acute perhaps to a fault, she has had a long and distinguished career, starting off at the huge Booz, Allen & Hamilton consultancy, later working in strategic planning and magazine development at Time, Inc., then for the past twenty years running her own firm. And while she modified and modulated her behavior over the years as a corporate employee, she ultimately believed those environments were destructive to her—primarily because she felt constrained from expressing her true emotional nature.

But even as an independent contractor her emotional involvement in her work continued to intrude on her efficacy. "Where I have gotten into trouble historically as a consultant," she said, "is [where] I find it's difficult to let go of something when I feel someone is making a significant error in judgment. I had one client tell me a year ago in an extremely unpleasant conversation that I get emotionally involved in the outcome, and that he thought I find it difficult to define the line of who's in charge." When Sandy feels very strongly that a mistake is being made and is unable to influence the outcome, her command-and-control systems have a tendency to fall short. "I have found I lose credibility as a result of the intensity with which I interact on that kind of an issue," she says. It's a dynamic that she's tried to manage, but one that has caused people to characterize her as inappropriately emotional in her dealings. Sandy's example illustrates how precarious the perceived line between conviction and aggression can be for women.

In 2007, Victoria Brescoll, an assistant professor at the Yale School of Management, and Eric Uhlmann, a postdoctoral research associate at the Kellogg School of Management at Northwestern University, conducted three studies in which people watched videos of male and female actors pretending to apply for jobs, and then assigned jobs and salaries to the make-believe new hires based on the behavior in the videos. The studies concluded that not only do women lose work-related status when they express anger but that men actually *gain* status. Data from our JWT Emotional Incidents in the Workplace Survey supports these findings: 42 percent of younger men believe that anger is an effective management tool.

Brescoll also reported that "women are just as likely as men to denigrate an angry woman." Whether the angry female in the experiments was described as a trainee or an executive, both men and women rated the angry woman lower because she showed anger. Additionally, the woman's anger was attributed to internal characteristics—"She is an angry person," "She is out of control"—whereas men's emotional reactions were ascribed to some external factor that seemed to justify anger—"The work was shoddy" or "The report sucked." The female faux-job-applicants were rated equal to men only when they expressed sadness, as opposed to anger.

If a woman only got angry, and expressed anger in a conventionally man-like fashion, that would be one thing. But often, angry women cry, with tears and blubbering as the unintended, rechannelled by-products of anger. Whether this is a result of the complex interplay of power within an organization, a reflection of cultural men-are-free-to-express-their-anger-while-women-are-not values, or a combination of both, when a person believes that he or she has been attacked but cannot show anger he or she either suppresses the feelings or, in the more classically female response, the anger is pushed down but tears immediately come out, Whac-a-Mole-style, like what happened to me during and after my call with Redstone.

In *Anger: The Misunderstood Emotion,* psychologist Carol Tavris writes that "because crying is not an act of aggression, tears are . . . a more socially acceptable act of self-preservation, allowing the employee to communicate their distress without being directly confrontational. The problem is[,] those kinds of tears are ineffectual, making neither the crier nor the observer feel good." Tavris cites studies that "have demonstrated that when we are denied the expression of what we believe is our *righteous* anger, we end up feeling powerless, and of lower status." And of course, because women are often actually in positions of lower status, this tends to deliver women a double dose of recrimination. According to Tavris, anger has potentially cathartic value only when expressed against peers or subordinates. If the target is your boss or an innocent bystander, you can wind up feeling worse. Most interesting, for *women,* "any aggression . . . was as arousing and upsetting as aggression toward authority was for the men." What *is* cathartic for women to express when they're angry, according to the research? *Friendliness.* Which of course, in addition to social conditioning, ties back to a woman's pituitary gland pumping out oxytocin, the bonding hormone, when she's under stress.

Anger does not occur as an isolated event. The emotion is context-specific, involving a complicated interplay between biology and culture. So a first step in more fully analyzing anger at work is to identify with greater precision the particular elements unique to a situation.

SCREAMERS

At the time Redstone ripped into me, I felt that I had been singled out for persecution. However, as part of the process of writing this book, I got in touch with several of my former colleagues from Nickelodeon and discovered that I was not at all unique in having been on the receiving end of Redstone's anger. Our biggest boss got angry promiscuously and almost indiscriminately. He yelled at people in private, in public, anywhere and everywhere. For all I know, he yells when he's by himself—which is an almost tautological definition of chronic anger.

"Sumner just had a different standard," recalled Harvey Ganot, the former head of MTV Network's ad sales. "I can remember a couple of times when I'd be in a meeting with him and he'd rant at me, 'Hey, call me back when you're making real money. What do you think this is, some kind of *hobby*?' "

Tom Freston, the chairman of MTV Networks at the time I worked there—and until Redstone fired him in 2006—wasn't at all surprised to learn that he had screamed at me. "Oh, yeah," he said, "I was screamed at by Redstone. You know, you find a lot of 'screamers' in the entertainment business, and Redstone could, at times, be a leading light in that regard." And what does Freston think was behind Redstone's anger? "His screaming, I think, is rooted in his difficulty to be able to connect with people in a healthy and empathetic way. His agenda overrode everything."

Redstone's behavior—using anger to assert power—offers a textbook example of what Jonah Lehrer discusses in *How We Decide,* his book about the neuroscience of important everyday behavior. Lehrer cites research by University of California Berkeley psychologist Dacher Keltner, who has found that people in positions of power can behave exactly like patients with a particular type of brain damage—as if the "part of [their] brain so critical to empathy and socially appropriate behavior" has been removed, making the powerful person more impulsive and insensitive. "[A]s a result, the inner Machiavelli takes over, and the sense of sympathy is squashed by selfishness."

But Machiavelli, at least, was all about self-serving *rationality.*

If you are working for a chronically angry person who seems to thrive on abusing others, you need to talk to other people you work with about your feelings and try to get their insight and support while you lay the foundation for your next job, because chronic, caustic anger always has a price. And that price is almost always your well-being. Interestingly, in our JWT Workplace Survey, 43 percent of the respondents had coped with anger episodes at work in precisely this way—by talking to a sympathetic colleague.

IT'S NOT ME, IT'S YOU

Anger in response to frustrations encountered on the job is one of the most pervasive kinds, with 69 percent of our survey respondents reporting having been frustrated during the past year. This sort of anger lets off steam and relieves stress, and almost half the people surveyed cited the perception of coworkers not doing their jobs properly as a prime motivator for frustration-driven anger.

Among the scores of conversations I had with people for this book, one of the most interesting was with a middle-aged project manager at a Fortune 500 telecommunications company in the Midwest who typified the kind of anger triggered by frustration. He was eager to talk but insisted that I give him a pseudonym, because he was concerned that he might lose his job for talking with me. I'll call him Ed White.

Some years ago, Ed was responsible for audio-recording the report of quarterly company earnings that went out by phone to stock-market analysts—a huge responsibility. The report was supposed to be released at 7:00 a.m., "not 6:59 and not 7:01," as he put it. On one of those quarterly D-days, Ed was notified at 7:10 that the report had not been issued. After a quick inquiry he determined that a woman in his department was responsible. "I started calling her and she didn't answer her phone," he told me, his voice growing agitated as he recalled the incident. "She was absent and I don't know why—I mean, this is a *phone* company, and the regulatory side of the company, which was supposed to respond quickly to things, and her lackadaisical attitude was inappropriate." Finally, at 10:30, three and half hours after they were supposed to release the information and after having been besieged by vice presidents and directors asking him why *he* couldn't get the job done, Ed reached his colleague. " 'Goddamn it!' " he remembers telling her. " 'This is your fucking job! Why don't you just get it done!' Now I understand that you don't tell people that in a business situation, but damn, sometimes you just have to light a fire and get something going. She hung up on me, and I just let it go and forgot about it, telling corporate that the info had gone out."

"Turns out," he said, "she'd gone to someone in my department, breaking down in tears and telling them I had been abusive to her." Ultimately Ed was reamed out by his boss and told to apologize, making *him* feel like the victim. "That was a game changer for me," he said, "I was the bad guy." Ed felt that the woman who had failed to do her job correctly was more seriously at fault than he, but because he was the one who lost his temper, he was the one punished. And while he felt that he was justified in his anger, how he chose to express it was not effective. As a long-time employee of the company, one would think he'd have had a better reading on what kind of emotional behavior was considered acceptable. But on the other hand, because companies and the culture at large have generally avoided the subject of emotion, with all its slippery unpredictability, and failed to establish clear protocols about emotional expression in the workplace,

Ed, like so many of us, was on his own, improvising, flailing, and failing.

Our reflexive horror at people who get angry at work, like Ed, is reflected in how our survey respondents labeled colleagues (labeled almost equally by women and men) whom they had observed getting angry. In descending order of importance, our respondents labeled people who got angry at work: unprofessional, overbearing, assertive, hostile, mean, immature, spiteful, out of control, malicious, crazy, weak, and violent. Clearly none of us would welcome these appraisals.

Twenty-four-year-old Jamee Lawson's situation illustrates how ineffectual anger is in motivating behavior and how negatively we view it at work, particularly when on the receiving end. Jamee, now an assistant account executive for the Ketchum advertising agency in Atlanta, has suffered at the hands of angry female bosses. In one instance, when her boss was unavailable, Jamee was forced to consult with other colleagues to find information necessary to complete an assignment—only to be lambasted by her boss for undermining her authority and, more critically, for letting others outside the department know that the boss wasn't there for her when she needed her. "I was really, really shocked, because I grew up in a house where we weren't yelled at, and no one had ever yelled at me before—and particularly not when I had done an excellent job completing the report."

The second time a boss inappropriately yelled at her felt even worse. Jamee was working for another woman, "one of those people who like to look busier than they are—you know, the come-in-early-and-stay-late kind of people who take the credit for other people's work. She'd groan and groan about how much work she had, and then would always ask for help at the last minute. She was also one of those sickeningly-sweet-on-the-outside, total-viper-on-the-inside kind of people." Jamee took on a last-minute assignment when she already had other priority assignments, and her boss called her on the phone, yelling that the work was not done correctly, and actually hung up on her. "I was so upset," Jamee said, "that I went to my manager, and my manager went to his boss, and [the superficially sweet viper] was finally told that that kind of behavior isn't acceptable."

WHEN PUSH COMES TO SHOVE

People who feel undervalued in their work—one in six of our survey respondents—are often the recipients of others' misplaced anger, and many shared stories similar to Paula Froelich's. Paula, a 33-year-old novelist and media personality, is one of the most extroverted, flagrantly expressive people I've ever met. She describes her last three years as deputy editor of the *New York Post*'s "Page Six" gossip column, from 2006 to 2009, as "the worst of my life." One of Paula's bosses came under attack, was scared for his job, and didn't behave very well—blaming anyone but himself for his poor performance. "He would just rip you a new asshole," said Paula, if anything went the slightest bit wrong.

It took her a long time to leave the job because she was "so frantic and anxious and furious and angsty that I didn't want to take just anything that came along," until one day her boss just started screaming, "I mean blood-vessels-were-popping kind of screaming." In that moment Paula realized that the stress of staying in the job was negatively affecting her health. The next day she woke up with clarity and said, "Enough. And I quit. The amount of money you are paying me and health insurance is not worth my being unhappy."

Instinctive self-preservation may have driven Paula's reciprocal fury and her need to take action. Perpetually bottled-up anger can actually make people sick. In 2009, the *Journal of Epidemiology and Community Health* reported findings from a study of

2,755 men conducted by the Stress Research Center at the University of Stockholm that concluded that there was a significant increase in coronary heart disease when an employee "does not show the 'aggressor' that he/she feels unfairly treated."

Daphne Poser knows how injurious to one's psychological well-being it can be to work in an environment shaped overall by aggressive, abusive behavior. She is a feminine and patrician 46-year-old working in an unusually macho world, as a coordinator of design, financing, and construction for major real estate projects in New York City. While lately she's encountering more women in her work, men continue to dominate the fields in which she operates. "A lot of these guys don't like to admit that they don't know something or that they are wrong—it's very traditional in that way. At the firm I used to work at, their approach to everything was very much 'the meanest apes in the jungle' and I was, you know, I was just *mean.*"

A lot of her perceived meanness could be attributed to the inherent stress of her particular job. "Because so much of my job is to absorb my client's tension—my role is to take their criticism and say 'You're right,' or 'Let me think about that,' and you never really know if they are yelling at you because you did something wrong or because they are upset. And with contractors you always get into shouting matches." That degree of chronic, high-volume tension takes a toll. Somewhat ironically, Daphne became angry at how she was treated in the company and feared that she was becoming an even angrier person at work and at home, something that was tolerable as long as she felt that the psychic investment would be professionally rewarded. When she was passed over for promotion, though, and a colleague she didn't respect was chosen instead, her anger boiled over.

"I was furious," she said, "I stomped around the office for days, actually throwing things at walls, muttering to myself. I made no secret of how I felt. I had worked very hard, long hours, weekends, putting personal pleasure aside so that I could devote myself to my job." Finally, she could take it no longer and asked to meet with the two senior partners to discuss why she hadn't been promoted. As she listened to them stumble around, failing to legitimize their choice, Daphne came to the conclusion that she was working for people who had no clue how to manage staff, nor any real knowledge of what was going on in their own company. "In an instant," she said, "I realized I had to leave. I couldn't work for people like that and in an atmosphere that had become poisonous for me." In other words, she didn't swallow her anger, or vent for its own sake, or ratchet up her own abuse of others, but instead took her anger as a powerful signal that she needed to make a change—and did so, finding a place to work where reasonable emotional regulation was more deeply embedded in the culture.

"My current boss says it took him a year to turn me back into a nice human," Daphne says. "I don't doubt it." Her boss kept reminding her that a collegial atmosphere is much more pleasant to work in and ultimately makes even the hardest projects easier to survive. "It's true," she says, "I now hate the kind of confrontations that used to roll off my back, and I'm appalled when I see other people behaving badly." Today if she needs to discipline someone, she does it in private. The new job is no less stressful or demanding because clients still expect their projects to be delivered on schedule and on budget with the highest quality their money can buy. And every project has different personalities to contend with but she is no longer seething with anger.

FROM BAD TO BETTER

Jim Cramer finally realized that he needed therapeutic help if he wanted some measure of contentment alongside his wealth. And he got the help he needed after he left full-time trading. "The issue, as I discovered too late for the people who worked with me at my fund, was medical, bipolar, and it is not something you control without help and medicine, and that's what I've been getting ever since the diagnosis. I sure wish I had known earlier. A lot of heartache for everyone could have been avoided."

Post-diagnosis, Jim has used the innovative format of his CNBC program, *Mad Money,* to channel his anger and other vivid emotions in a productive way that no longer leaves bodies in his wake. And he's developed anger-control skills that have been tested in very public ways, most spectacularly during his 2009 appearance on *The Daily Show,* on which Jon Stewart booked Jim in order to make him the poster boy for both CNBC's uncritical treatment of Wall Street during the bubble and the meltdown generally. The experience was painful for Jim, but he was happy that during the broadcast he was able to think rationally versus irrationally. He realized that "I could use the Stewart thing as a learning moment—I love my show and don't want to embarrass myself in terms of creating my own hurt." Stewart was hell-bent on being a prosecutor, wanting to provoke the old angry hedge-fund Jim, but when provoked by Stewart, Jim thought, " 'Let's think rationally about this. If I hit Stewart over the head, I get fired and I lose my show. If I do something really dramatic, I put a lot of things in jeopardy that I really love.' So I took the beating and moved on. I don't need to be lifelong enemies with anybody anymore. I've enough of them to last me a lifetime already." Through therapy and concerted effort Jim is now able to stop and think about the consequences of his actions and therefore be more effective. Jim has struggled very hard "not to be a hothead and not to be petulant, because those are traits I've had. And [the *Daily Show* appearance] was a true test of who I'm trying to be."

In other words: *Let's think rationally about this.* By stepping back, and objectively assessing what was at stake, Jim modeled successful anger management. He recognized his issue, got medical help, and works consciously at modifying his behavior, demonstrating that while, yes, it's always personal, each of us has power over how we choose to respond to life's emotional twists and turns.

If you regularly experience volcanic rage and think your workplace behavior might resemble Jim Cramer's in his hedge-fund days, find a therapist. And if you work for someone like the hedge-fund-era Cramer, where the level of anger veers into degrading abuse, it might be worth discussing with others how you can stage an intervention—or an escape. But one doesn't need to be facing a diagnosis like Jim's to benefit from counseling or medication. I sought the advice of Paul Browde, a psychiatrist and assistant clinical professor at NYU's School of Medicine, who says that many of his patients, particularly women, come to him for help dealing with their emotions at work, and "there is no question that there are plenty of people for whom psychotropic medicines are indeed beneficial." According to Browde, unrestrained expressions of emotion can be symptoms of anxiety or depressive disorders that can be effectively treated with antidepressant and anti-anxiety medications. However, Browde cautions that these medications, "can also achieve the result of suppressing emotional expression in the workplace in people who are not clinically depressed." He's more than a bit concerned that such drugs can work as a Band-Aid in a bad way to the extent that they block people from facing their feelings and dealing with the underlying logistical or personality issues. "I am not sure that it is ultimately helpful for a woman to have legitimate expressions of anger, fear, and disappointment suppressed so that she can appear more 'appropriate' in the workplace. What message does this send to her psyche? One that over time could devalue her self-esteem."

This notion is central to our conversation about anger. Of course, discerning when a person will benefit from medication is the job of a trained therapist, but the key task is trying to strike the right balance—between assertively responding and defensively coping as a recipient, and between effective motivation and gratuitously brutal venting as a perpetrator. In medically diagnosed instances such as Cramer's, drug therapies can be lifesaving. In others they can mute signals that would be useful tools for self-reflection and, perhaps, impetus to change one's life in important ways or at the minimum to seek a different job.

WHY UNDERSTANDING ANGER CAN BE GOOD FOR BUSINESS AND GOOD FOR YOU

Although we live in a culture filled with anger, and in spite of the fact that most people think the expression of emotion at work can be a positive force, my research with JWT clearly reveals that the *exception* to this rule is *anger.* None of us like it when faced with angry men or women at work. And more often than not, anger itself is not good for business. Angry work environments don't make people snap to and work well together, but rather drive good people away.

Understanding how we *process* anger—our own and others'—is helpful in learning how to deal with it on the job. If women understand that men are wired by nature to be more aggressive—with more of their behavior driven by the more primitive part of their brains, the amygdala, and the secretion of epinephrine and cortisol—then male anger should become less disturbing for them. We would know not to take it so personally. If women more clearly understand why they experience a double-whammy speedball when they get angry—that the oxytocin in their bodies is in conflict with the norepinephrine that they also produce when under attack—then they might be less negatively judgmental about their own and other women's anger. If both genders realize that, as Browde says, "the suppression of an emotional response to being demeaned and belittled in the workplace has physiologic effects and can result in symptoms such as insomnia, irritability, anxiety, panic, and even depression," then all of us might try harder not to upset each other. And if women's biologically driven default approach is to seek a collaborative solution, then as the American workplace becomes more and more a female place, it follows that there might be fewer dysfunctionally angry outbursts.

BUILDING YOUR ANGER EMOTION MANAGEMENT TOOLKIT

As I mentioned at the end of Chapter Two, and beginning here, I offer a variety of strategies for managing difficult workplace emotions. Different people respond to different situations differently, and while you may be able to shrug off anger at your colleague, you may not be able to do the same for your boss or vice versa. But you do need to learn how to handle anger in the workplace, so think about the EMTs that follow, select those that seem to resonate, try them in practice, and, if you find them helpful, begin to build a repertoire of strategies that you can call upon during times of stress.

EMT—CHANGING PERSPECTIVE

If you find yourself being aggressively berated by someone like Jim, Sumner, or Ed, you might benefit from a little trick I've developed over the years since Redstone so upset me. It sounds silly, but it can also be helpful in the moment. If someone is screaming at you, reimagine them as a 2-year-old. Literally. If I experience outrageous behavior from "professionals," it is much easier to let their anger roll off my back by shrinking them in my mind to the image of a spoiled brat having a temper tantrum. Try it. Imagine your shouting boss right now as a shrieking little toddler and with any luck, the notion will make you laugh and the moment will pass. Equally effective as a way to put inappropriate anger in its place is to imagine the screamer *melting* away—something like what happened when Dorothy threw water on the Wicked Witch of the West in *The Wizard of Oz.*

EMT—WHEN IS IT OKAY TO GET ANGRY?

Daphne Poser, the New York City construction coordinator, offers a great example for how directed anger can be an effective catalyst and tool for change. In *Anger: The Misunderstood Emotion,* Carol Tavris notes that in order for the expression of anger to be effective, four criteria must be met: (1) the anger must be directed at the target of your anger; (2) the expression of anger must restore your sense of control over the situation and your sense of justice; it must inflict appropriate harm on the other person; (3) the expression of anger must change the behavior of the target or give you new insights; and (4) you and your target must speak the same anger language. Daphne appropriately directed her anger at her former bosses who were incapable of articulating the reasons she'd been passed over for promotion. By asking for the meeting, she took control of the situation, and the exchange allowed her to gain new insight into her situation and her values, leading her to change her life.

EMT—HOW TO LET SOMEONE KNOW YOU'RE ANGRY

There are indeed times and places for workplace anger if it's properly—that is, *rationally*—directed and managed. "What is terrifying for a lot of people at work," Paul Browde says, "is uncontained and undirected rage." He also says that it's important *not* to engage the person at whom one feels anger in the heat of the moment. Instead of waiting for the dam to burst spontaneously, open your floodgates strategically. Rather than confronting someone in the hallway immediately after they've ticked you off, Browde suggests setting up a meeting with the person in a private space. The meeting time establishes a boundary and the private room establishes a container so that the conversation will have a greater chance of achieving a constructive outcome—and of allowing a productive ongoing relationship to be maintained. He recommends starting the conversation by asking the other person involved if they are willing to listen, explaining that you have something important to say. He also advises that if the meeting doesn't go as planned, since "there are some people who just cannot tolerate that kind of open communication," you don't blame yourself for the failure.

EMT—WHAT IF I LET LOOSE AND THEN REGRET IT? HOW TO APOLOGIZE

If you've ever blown up at someone inappropriately, there are plenty of options to redress what you perceive as your wrong behavior, but a simple apology is a good first step. With no excuses. No apology will work if it is accompanied by a self-referential caveat: *I'm sorry I yelled at you, Kate, but I'm just so anxious about my project, and I feel so much pressure, and you know I've been sick,* etc., etc. That kind of apology is all about *you* and not the person you hurt, and as a result it will feel insincere. Instead, simply say, *I'm sorry I yelled at you, Kate. It was inexcusable. I will try not to let it happen again.* I know this seems very basic, but somehow it is a lesson I need to remind myself of over and over again.

The best way to make an apology sound genuine is to have it *be* genuine. "Sometimes it's hard to access feeling sorry, as you are still bruised and a little dazed from the day before," Paul Browde says. "So think about the effect of your actions on the other person, and recognize how it must have made them feel, and the consequences of your behavior. Facing those consequences will perhaps allow you to feel compassion for the person you were so angry at the day before." According to Browde, "it takes humility and courage to apologize, so saying 'I am sorry for the way I behaved' can help you to feel sorry for the way you behaved. The action of apology may precede the feeling of being sorry."

Saying you're sorry is not enough. Browde recommends that you "listen and see if there's anything *they* want to say. If they then tell you how hurt or angry they felt in response to your outburst, do not justify your behavior from the day before, rather listen and receive their communication, take deep breaths and just take it in. That will often defuse the whole situation. Apologize and then listen, do not defend, do not react, just listen. That is key. Less is more."

Browde also had useful advice for dealing with our individual negative feedback loops. "Once you have apologized, notice that beating yourself up for 'being out of control' is using the aggressive language you're trying to move away from to punish yourself. Just let go. Also derive a sense of self-esteem from your ability to take responsibility for your behavior and your humility in being able to apologize for treating another human being the way that you did. Now don't treat yourself in the same way."

EMT—METACOGNITION, OR LEARNING TO STEP BACK

One essential skill in building greater emotional intelligence is metacognition, or the ability to step back and think about ourselves thinking and reacting. Many experts suggest that one think about anger, going toward it rather than away from it, because if one suppresses anger, there is a risk that it will find its way out in a more destructive manner. I developed my own tool for helping me understand and then face my anger—a mnemonic aid that I call DING that was inspired by the acronym Alcoholics Anonymous teaches to help people resist the temptation to drink

(HALT, for hungry, angry, lonely, and tired). I know it sounds a little goofy, but it works for me, and maybe it will work for you. When you feel like you might explode, try hearing a little bell go "ding" in your mind and then:

D—Deep breaths; take a few. The pause gives you time to think and the deep breathing activates your parasympathetic nervous system, which calms our bodies during stress.

I—Imagine what the other person is feeling, then identify what you are feeling. Are you on the same wavelength, or coming at the issue from irreconcilable points of view? Imagining yourself on the other side of the argument can provide insight into what is driving the anger.

N—Name the emotions you and the other person are feeling. If you are feeling fear in response to the other person's anger, explain that. They may well be totally unaware of your subjective situation. If you are angry, figure out why—are you jealous, resentful, exhausted, or unappreciated? Being specific and naming what you are feeling is important.

G—Go on. Having taken a moment to reflect, use your observations to move the situation forward.

FOUR

On Being Afraid

Let us not look back in anger, or forward with fear, but around in awareness. —James Thurber

Psychiatrist Paul Browde has firsthand experience with living in a continuous spirit-sucking state of fear—maybe that's why he's so good at helping others think about their difficult emotional states. In 1985 at the age of 24, Paul had just graduated from medical school and was doing an internship in medicine, surgery, and ob-gyn at a hospital in South Africa when he discovered that he was HIV-positive, which at that time was so little understood—particularly in South Africa, where he's from—that he felt compelled to keep it completely secret. "It was way too dangerous to speak about in those days," he said. "I was the first person I knew in South Africa to receive the diagnosis, and at the time it was a death sentence."

And so Paul was beset by the ultimate, existential fear—of a grisly, painful death.

The only knowledge Paul had of the condition came through gay friends in the United States, who were losing close members of their community every week. His way of dealing was to keep his diagnosis a secret from all but his mother, an oncologist. "Keeping it a secret," he said, "was a way of hiding the terrifying fact not only from others, but from myself, too. I think that I went into a state of denial, which allowed me to get through each day. I lived in a perpetual state of fear, with intermittent panic attacks. My friends found me cold and aloof, but I could not tell them why."

Paul found himself living under punishing stress, trapped in the feedback loop from hell—his reasonable fear of dying activated all his normal fight-or-flight physical responses, but the mysteriousness to the medical community of this wholly new infection meant that there was no medical course of treatment available. "People were dying," he said, "and the only public rhetoric was one of blame and judgment."

Since fighting was not an option, he fled, at first figuratively and then literally. "Thinking I had little time left spurred me to think about what I wanted to do with my remaining years. I decided to pursue my lifelong dream of training to be an actor. I was accepted to a drama school in London. I finished drama school and still, astoundingly, I was not sick. I tried working as an actor for a while, but soon realized what a difficult profession it was, humiliating and frustrating." Once the existential threat and its attendant fears seemed to recede, he had the luxury of experiencing small-caliber emotions like frustration.

Paul decided to return to medicine and this time chose to enter a psychiatric residency program in New York, keeping his health status a secret throughout his training. "There are many reasons I did this," he said, "including not wanting to shatter my own denial, but also fearing that I would lose my career as a psychiatrist. I could not imagine [that] anybody would willingly see a psychiatrist who was HIV-positive." At that time the stigma was great, and he'd heard how other doctors spoke about AIDS patients, saying that "they would never share a glass with one of those patients. I heard a senior doctor refer to an AIDS patient as a 'SHPOS,' which stood for 'subhuman piece of shit.' " If his medical colleagues called people like him *subhuman pieces of shit,* imagine how frightened he was that they might discover his secret.

WHAT IS FEAR?

What Paul has experienced, while extreme, can happen to any of us—a cancer diagnosis or the loss of a job—and offers insights into fear in all its Hydra-headed aspects. Evolutionary biology explains how some emotions undoubtedly served our ancestors as emergency neural software designed to enhance their ability to avoid fatal situations and reproduce more. To survive and thrive we had to respond to threats *first,* and according to what's known as negative bias, which says that our brains are wired to perceive potential *risks* more intensely than other situations—a pouncing leopard, a crumbling cliff edge—because survival depends on the split-second "startle" ability of our brains to infer threat and mount an instantaneous defense. Danger, either physical or emotional, bypasses the reasoning parts of our brains and hits us on the most primal level.

Joseph LeDoux, a New York University psychologist and a leading expert in the neuroscience of emotion, describes "two pathways through which the amygdala's fear responses can be triggered: a fast 'low road' from the thalamus [the part of the brain that relays sensory information to other parts of the brain] to the amygdala, and a slower 'high road' that passes from the thalamus to the neocortex"—the newer part of the brain, responsible for conscious thought, language, and spatial reasoning—"and only then to the amygdala. The two paths do not always reach the same conclusions. The relatively crude 'low road' [will] respond to a long, thin object as a dangerous snake—and trigger an immediate fear response—while the slower 'high road' is determining that the object is a harmless stick. Evolutionarily speaking, it may make sense for the faster pathway to err on the side of caution," LeDoux writes, since, after all, "it's probably better to treat a stick as a snake than a snake as a stick." But as LeDoux and others have discovered, the neural connections going *from* the predator-predicting part of our brain, the amygdala, *to* the more cognitively developed and memory-governing parts of our brain, the prefrontal cortex and the hippocampus, are very robust—so once an emotional reaction is activated, our cortex takes some time to turn it off.

At work, this hyperactivation happens on a daily if not hourly basis when negotiating complex social interactions. While the fears that one might screw up a deal, be passed over for promotion, or drop an overloaded tray while busing tables are not literally ones where life and death hang in the balance—although a layoff resulting in loss of health insurance *can* amount to such an existential threat—the twenty-first-century dangers we regularly face on the job are not innocuous sticks in the road, either. While our fear of the snake was intended to make us kill or run from it, fear at work often has no analogously obvious solution. The control mechanisms in our brains simply have not had time to develop appropriate behavioral responses to the subtler, primarily psychological kinds of snakes—the explosive boss, the aggressive colleague gunning for our job, the sense that technology is outstripping our skills, or the specter of "downsizing"—that pop up to scare us in the modern workplace.

WHEN THE SNAKE BECOMES OBVIOUS

Paul Browde's fear of exposure (and sickness and death) continued, made synergistically worse by his devotion to secrecy, for the better part of a decade, until his secret was discovered. "In my last year of residency, a patient who was seeing me for psychotherapy, a young male nursing student, told me that he had randomly [this being the era before secure password protection] come across my blood results on the hospital's computer. He discovered that I was HIV-positive and maliciously began to torment me. Week after week he came back and asked me how I felt knowing I was going to die. He asked if I would be kicked out of the program if he told my supervisors." Paul began having serious panic attacks. "Sometimes driving home from the Bronx, I would have to stop the car on the side of the road and wait half an hour for the panic to pass. I could not drive on bridges or in tunnels without massive outpourings of adrenaline and the fear that I was going to die. During conversations with supervisors I would watch them disappear into a long tunnel as the world went silent, except for the blood pounding in my head."

Keeping even relatively innocuous secrets is stressful; Paul's was beyond endurance. Finally, all of the compounded fears drove Paul to honesty. "I decided to go public with my story at the 1994 American Psychiatric Association's annual conference, and deliver a paper called 'The HIV-Positive Psychiatrist, Clinical Issues.' "

"I have now been HIV-positive for twenty-five years," says Paul, "and the greatest benefit of telling my story has been the ability to be my whole self in all areas of my life, including the workplace, which has dramatically lessened my anxiety, and I believe has had a role in keeping me well for so long. I have come to learn much from this process, including the realization that difficult circumstances are not life going *wrong,* but rather that they *are* life."

While nobody would want to endure what Paul Browde did, particularly at such a young age, how he chose to deal with his fears can offer those of us who find ourselves frightened in ways big or small some guidance. On the most primal level, Paul had to deal with the biggest fear of all—one's own suffering and prospective death—and in his case, his fear was magnified enormously by widespread fears of contagion. While it would have been better if Paul hadn't felt paralyzed by his additional fears of ostracization, by keeping his secret for a decade he perhaps unwittingly stumbled into a strategy that allowed him time to process his emotions in stages. He could come to terms with his condition without the added burden of dealing with rejection from his colleagues. Keeping his condition secret may also have offered him the illusion of control over a life that had been hijacked by something overwhelmingly beyond his control. By sharing his secret with his mother, someone he trusted implicitly, he allowed himself to benefit from the power of his social relationships and empathy. And by facing and acknowledging the biggest fear, death, he was able to use his hyperaroused state to find greater meaning in the life remaining to him.

WHEN THE SNAKE IS A PERSON

If I were a schoolteacher, I'd want Lisa Elliott to be my advocate. As executive director of the Jefferson County Education Association, a teachers' union in suburban Denver, she works on behalf of the 5,400 teachers in the largest school district in Colorado. But she didn't start out looking to become a labor organizer or activist. Like many of us, Lisa found herself floundering slightly after college, moving from job to job. She'd done all of the things "you're supposed to do" to try to find meaningful work—reading the books, talking to people in various industries, but "all of those jobs just seemed really unimportant to me." She happened upon a Help Wanted ad for a job as an English teacher at her old high school in Kansas City, Missouri. "When I saw the ad I just knew that teaching was something important and something I wanted to do."

For the next sixteen years, Lisa taught English to grades 7 to 11, and found real value in her work. But as much as she loved teaching, she also found herself afraid a lot of the time—not because of worries about her skills or her students, but because so many of her administrators were "petty, small-minded people who tended to rule their fiefdoms through shame and intimidation." One stint was particularly demoralizing. "For years I worked in an environment that was just draining," she says. "It got so bad that if I drove into the parking lot in the morning and my principal's car was already there, I'd feel a huge knot in my stomach because I knew I'd have to deal with him." He was, she says, a "micromanaging bully who denied his teachers any leeway for independent professional judgment about how or what to teach." And while Lisa had the security of a contract, the principal could still intimidate teachers in any number of demeaning ways. "If you found yourself on the wrong side of him," Lisa says, "you could find yourself teaching kindergarten, or he could put you on a schedule where you had to teach in three or four classrooms, or he could move your class. We lived in a constant state of fear, a drip, drip, drip, where we felt he questioned our every move—taking the student or parent's word in any situation." Fortunately for Lisa, she was able to transfer to another school, and slowly her confidence and satisfaction returned.

WHEN THE SNAKE IS A MOVING TARGET—IT'S THE ECONOMY, STUPID

During the last couple of decades, and particularly during the Great Recession, to work has been to live with a perpetual sense of vulnerability, even for those of us who don't face death on the job. Much more than for Americans in the 1950s, 60s, and 70s, the economic rug may be pulled out from under each of us at any moment. As Cathy Hamilton, a 55-year-old journalist from Lawrence, Kansas, put it, "If you're a journalist in 2010 and you're *not* scared, you've already checked out or you're completely delusional. I get scared practically every time the CEO calls a company meeting. In December, it was to announce across-the-board pay cuts, and the year before it was a pay freeze. I'm a valued employee and have twenty years with the company but I still get scared." And who can blame Cathy? During the past few years most of us have learned to acclimate to pay cuts, required "furloughs," dwindling 401ks, escalating insurance costs, and the prospect that as we age we will have to work longer and harder than we'd anticipated to reach at best a radically downsized expectation of what retirement will mean. Many of us face this uncertainty while sandwiched between dealing with our increasingly expensive-to-care-for aging parents and trying to cover the skyrocketing everyday expenses of raising kids and carrying mortgages. The tiniest change in status is enough to implode the sense of security of even the most confident of us. To say that thinking about work in the future is scary is an understatement.

Karen Rosenthal, a California-based executive coach for more than twenty years, believes that "there is a great paralysis up and down in most organizations these days around the notion of 'when is the pink slip going to hit me?' The fear is so pervasive and people are so maxed out and inward-focused on their own issues that they are not listening to the external cues about what's happening. This sense that our expectations will become reality is really dangerous for a company and for individuals because it slows everything down, stopping productivity and innovation, and when people are fearful they aren't performing at their best levels."

REAL AND PRESENT DANGER

Tom Casey, a former American Airlines captain, worked in a profession where fear operated in much the same way that it has for many years in other occupations. The 59-year-old Casey looks and acts like a pilot from Central Casting, ruggedly handsome, confident, and articulate—Harrison Ford could play him in the movie of his life. "Pilots," he says, "are like surfers or rodeo riders, stamped with that adrenaline challenge to fly the big machine, all that old 'Right Stuff.' " And like surfers or rodeo riders, they can obviously find themselves in immediate, potentially catastrophic danger.

Not long after 9/11, Tom was in command of a Boeing 777 flight to London from New York City, "when what felt like an explosion in the cargo compartment forced an emergency diversion." While I was imagining the panic I would have felt in such a situation, Tom proceeded to explain how he had assessed the level of danger, without panicking. Immediately, he got verification from his first officer and flight attendants throughout the aircraft that everyone had heard the same sound. Then he says, "My mind accelerated and there was an impression of time slowing down. I took the plane off autopilot to feel its undisguised flight control."

Tom discovered no anomalies, no indications of fire, and no loss of pressurization. That was the good news. And the bad? He had to tell Air Traffic Control that he had an undetermined problem and request "a rapid descent to 10,000 feet and a direct course to Gander [in Canada] for landing." Tom also asked for emergency personnel to stand by and a straight-in approach. In the back of his mind was an incident from a few years earlier when a Swiss Air jet had crashed after a fire broke out in the cockpit and a contributing cause had been slow pilot response to a rapidly deteriorating condition. "That wasn't going to happen to me," he said. "But we were in uncertain circumstances. Acid could be eating through the fuselage, or a fire could be burning out of control." Any airborne emergency must be handled methodically, one step at a time and yet in a rapid-fire process. Through his decades of experience he knew that "a low altitude would eliminate concerns about depressurization. I deployed the speed brake to increase drag and hasten descent. I instructed the first officer to notify the cabin crew of our intentions and then made a PA to the passengers advising them of an imminent precautionary landing. We ran appropriate checklists. The runway appeared in front of us, brightly lit." And Tom landed the plane without incident.

"Specialists were flown up from JFK," he said, "and we soon identified the problem—a box of construction parts had fallen against a cargo bin with a huge crash. The worst had not happened, but my crew and I had lived through a real-time, real-world threat."

Looking back on that post-9/11 night and his response, Tom was not surprised that he had almost immediately found what sounded like his Zen center. "The acceleration of thinking and performance came naturally," he said, "with sharp focus on necessities." Tom responded to events as they presented themselves and took action to avoid unnecessary problems while keeping in mind dire possibilities.

According to Tom, one way he manages his fear is to define the peril as precisely as possible. Is a threat real or imagined, and how should it be treated? He believes that success at *anything* is about having "situational awareness," which is the ability to perceive and interpret a variety of environmental elements within the context of a specific time and place and to then make a projection based on those observations about what will occur in the near future. To Tom this means deciding which fears should be your *legitimate* concerns. "As a pilot, alone at night in the weather," he says, "I have been keenly aware of my fears," and those threat-detecting emotions can spring more easily from a bed of ambient anxiety. "A person governed by anxiety," Tom says, "will tend to project peril and be prone to irrational response." Conversely, "a person not overly influenced by inner fears will do a rational appraisal of external considerations but may underestimate irrational factors and be surprised by them." Most of us are a combination of these two types. We must always be in conference with our emotions and their sources to accord them a proper authority. Healthy fear keeps police officers, doctors, and pilots properly on alert: too much fear paralyzes action and can compromise performance.

BUILDING YOUR FEAR EMOTION MANAGEMENT TOOLKIT

As discussed at the end of Chapter Three, developing greater skill in managing seemingly conflicting impulses entails strengthening our metacognition. Here are a few more developmental strategies to explore.

EMT—IMPROVING SITUATIONAL AWARENESS

Developing greater fluency in the kind of situational awareness that Tom Casey mentioned has gained traction over the past few decades as a mental habit that can give a competitive advantage to people working in businesses like aviation, air traffic control, emergency services, and power plants. In businesses like these, where the complexity of operations is dynamic and increasingly automated yet where the accuracy of an individual's split-second decision-making also bears potentially drastic consequences, it can mean the difference between life and death. It is also a skill that can benefit many of us in myriad work environments.

If we are made fearful by the anticipation of an event for

which we feel underqualified or underprepared—I'll be fired if I admit that I don't understand the assignment, I won't get promoted if I don't know how to run the inventory, or I have no idea how to develop a new list of prospects—then the more each of us can develop an objective, fact-based sense of all aspects of our work environment, a situational-awareness analysis as it were, the more successful we might become at minimizing fears that deserve minimizing.

At the most basic level, situational awareness is knowing what's going on around you. By simply articulating that you know you need to develop specific skills to advance in your job you can proactively identify courses to take, or request specific instruction from your supervisor. In my experience, no boss minds helping an eager employee learn something new or develop her skills, but every boss resents having to intervene in a bungled project because an employee was afraid to be honest about gaps in her skill set.

I encourage you to conduct your own "situational-awareness analysis" twice a year. First and foremost, ask how you are feeling. Are you challenged? Cowering from a scary boss? Overburdened and anxious? Bored? In your analysis, identify to the best of your ability the skills you have, the skills that your colleagues and bosses have, and where you might fall short. Do your peers seem to be developing skills at a faster rate than you? From your analysis, is there any one thing that sets someone you admire within your company apart from the others? If so, what is it? Is it something that you can acquire or enhance by taking a course? Is the industry changing in ways that require new training? Is your company not doing things that its competitors are doing? And it's very important that you don't lock yourself into one interpretation right off the bat. Situational awareness is not only about observing things around you—it's also about *interpreting* the information based on experience. Try thinking about the circumstances from different vantage points, and new insights might emerge.

Let's take someone working in an industry I know well as an example. Imagine a mid-level editor at a general interest magazine in the early 2000s. A situational-awareness analysis at that time would have revealed that she was feeling anxious: increased manufacturing costs tied to paper production and distribution expenses were dramatically cutting into operating margins; new digital media were reducing sources of traditional advertising revenue; and younger, far-less-expensive employees with more fluency in digital technology were offering competition and new expertise to management. But rather than feeling paralyzed by one's fear, this kind of process can lead to nimble reactions and flexible thinking. The result, in this hypothetical case, might have provoked the editor to join a new media team within her company, could have inspired her to start reading blogs to keep up with changes in the business in a more proactive way, could have motivated her to talk to her boss about her concerns, or could even have inspired her to envision creating a beta program for transitioning the print content of her magazine to the Web. Each of these strategies would have offered her positive outcomes and would have effectively helped the editor manage her fears.

EMT—ASK FOR HELP

As human beings, most of us are wired to help others in distress, as home observational studies of infants by Carolyn Zahn-Waxler and Marian Radke-Yarrow for the National Institute of Mental Health indicate. Over a nine-month period they observed children from 10 months to 20 months old responding to naturally occurring expressions of emotion around them. The researchers discovered that even among the youngest of the kids, when someone around them signaled distress, the infants oriented themselves toward that person. As they developed social skills, at about age 1, they began touching or patting the distressed person, and as older infants they demonstrated even more constructive behavior like seeking an adult's help or offering verbal assurances. In the dog-eat-dog competitive fray of the workplace it is easy to forget this basic component of human behavior. We like to help others. So if you feel overwhelmed remember this and ask for help.

The benefit of reaching out to others for help is supported by findings from a recent Dutch longitudinal study of adolescents who kept secrets. The researchers established that keeping important secrets contributed to all sorts of psychosocial problems—low self-concept, loneliness, a depressive mood—but when the adolescents—as Paul Browde also discovered—shared their secret, allowing others to help them, many of those symptoms were alleviated.

EMT—BUILD SELF-CONFIDENCE

While Lisa Elliott ultimately lucked out when she was able to transfer away from her fearmongering boss, before the opportunity arose she discovered a highly unusual route to renew her sense of purpose in her job—one that might be beneficial for others feeling threatened by abusive superiors. In the course of therapy to deal with her depression, Lisa began to explore her history of childhood physical abuse, which, in turn, led her to participate in a women's self-defense program called Model Mugging. The intensive weekend-long course was designed to help women in particular overcome their fears of being assaulted. But in addition to developing a sense of physical empowerment, for Lisa it also provided "a deep-seated self-confidence on a professional level. I don't enjoy conflict and I really don't enjoy people yelling at me, and the course offered me access to an inner place of strength."

Taking the course and ultimately becoming a Model Mugging instructor herself, she says, enabled her to feel, in dealing with her bad boss, that she was no longer "scared of him when he was raising his voice. It really impacted my professional life, which eventually led me to becoming a staff person with my teachers' association." Now, as she says, "my job is to protect the underdog." Lisa's experience vividly illustrates what I've said about the connections between our ancient biological selves and very different modern circumstances: in her case, feeling prepared to deal with the fear that evolved as a response to physical threat enabled her to cope with the fear of human predators whose threats are social, psychological, and economic.

If Model Mugging feels too extreme for you, there are many different routes to develop greater self-confidence. When I was beginning to do publicity for my first book, for instance, I worked with Isabelle Anderson, a leadership coach, to help me overcome my fear of public speaking. Isabelle, an accomplished actor, trained with the late Jacques Lecoq, who established a nontraditional theater school in Paris that taught students to free their creative and emotional expression using the body as the primary vehicle. Over fifteen years Isabelle has developed a program to help business leaders build a more powerful public presence through their communication skills. According to Isabelle, when under stress, fearful people tend to close themselves up, camouflaging their true selves behind muffled voices and shrinking bodies. Her coaching is designed to do the opposite—to help people open themselves and expand their presence. She immediately diagnosed my particular issues, and over the course of several sessions taught me to become more comfortable with public speaking. In my case, according to Isabelle, "the face was the battleground of fear." She noticed that I could say "It was lots of fun writing this book" while my face was tight-lipped, serious, and shut like a drawbridge. No emotion expressed at all. From her perspective the audience would feel a disconnect between what I was saying and how I was expressing it.

Through a series of exercises to limber my facial muscles—raising my eyebrows; grinning and scowling; and moving my eyes up, down, and around—I was able to make my face more malleable and thus show a greater range of emotional expression. Isabelle also gave me exercises to loosen my flattened voice, for example, saying out loud several times a day "red leather, yellow leather" while distinctly articulating each word. Trust me, it's harder to do than you'd think. She also taught me breathing exercises, rehearsed various kinds of interview situations with me, and taught me how to project my voice and gestures to a large room. According to Isabelle, all her work is about owning your space. The contractions created in the body by stress and fear end up pushing you into a tiny space, like a bug under a microscope. Her work gives you back your space, and gives you solid ground and the ability to command the camera or the whole room. And I was surprised by what happened as a result of doing something as simple as expanding my vocal range and increasing the flexibility of my face. I began to feel more confident. Today I run through her techniques before I go into any meeting or presentation.

If neither of these approaches feels right for you, think about what might be behind your fears—perhaps improving your tennis or golf game would foster an improved sense of self-confidence. One woman I know decided at age 40 to learn how to ice-skate. Today she's the goalie for a regional women's ice hockey team and projects a refreshing degree of self-confidence in all other areas of her life. There are many different ways to improve self-confidence, and you can experiment with several—learn to knit, teach kids in an afterschool program, go skydiving, take a defensive driving course, finish Sunday crossword puzzles—what is important is to follow a personal interest or passion to find *at least* one activity that helps you feel good about yourself. That enhanced sense of self-confidence will carry over into your work life.

EMT—VALUE COURAGE

When we're frightened it's next to impossible for us to work at our optimal performance levels. It's scary to stick our necks out and rock the boat during particularly troubled economic times. But surprisingly, one of the best antidotes to fear at work is courage. Or as Lieutenant John B. Putnam, Jr., a young Air Force pilot during World War II, put it, "Courage is not the lack of fear but the ability to face it." In *Emotions in the Workplace,* the editors describe nineteenth-century psychologist William James's notion of courage as "energizing the will to allow people to face fear," and his idea that "courage gave humanity the ability to persist against the unknown."

I encourage you to think about any recent time when you felt that you, or someone you work with, did something courageous at work. It doesn't need to be anything monumental. Did you ask for your boss to clarify a complicated point in front of others? Did you ask a difficult customer to back off? How did it make you feel? Did you feel empowered afterward? Did the situation change? Did anyone stand up for you or another colleague during a contentious exchange? Do you think you might have been able to do something similar? If not, why not? What might it take for you to develop the confidence to do so?

I sometimes screw up my courage to do something scary while working by using a mantra that came to me a few years ago after an unpleasant experience on a crowded New York City morning rush-hour subway car. On this particular ride, a woman at the far end of the car was repeatedly slapping a crying 5- or 6-year-old child, and as I debated whether to intervene, I found myself imagining: *What would Michael Rips do?* Michael, a longtime friend and a lawyer by training, is also a deeply imaginative and philosophical writer of thoughtful autobiographical books, and seems completely unafraid to intertwine himself in strangers' lives. He courageously embraces and celebrates quirky, messy humanity, he has a huge capacity for empathy and humor, and he is flexible about life in ways that I wish I were. He is a constant inspiration.

On the subway, as the woman kept slapping and the child kept sobbing, I realized that Michael would have intervened to try to defuse the situation—perhaps he would have strolled casually up to the woman and started talking about how smart the little boy seemed or maybe he would have said, "Excuse me, I couldn't help noticing your shoes. My wife has been looking for a pair just like them. Might I ask where you found them?" What he said wouldn't have really mattered. What did matter is that he would have known how to neutralize a tough situation with charm. While I couldn't imagine precisely what I was going to say, I mustered my courage and decided to try to divert the woman's anger. As I made my way to her end of the subway car, another man beat me to it—although he handled the exchange with less grace than I'd imagined Michael doing. Mercifully, the woman nonetheless transferred her attention to the stranger and stopped slapping the little kid, turning her vitriol onto the Good Samaritan. "I dare *you* to tell *me* how to act!" she shouted. "I dare you!" It was scary, to say the least. I realized that this man could use some moral support in a highly charged situation, so I went to stand by him. The reaction of our fellow passengers could have been the New York City stereotype—"Who do you think you are to meddle in someone else's business?"—but because the man had defused a situation that was making everyone extremely uncomfortable, and because I believe my presence had lent additional weight to his intervention, the collective mood of the train was supportive. One man's actions dynamically changed a stressful situation. And by stepping outside my habitual perspective and suppressing my natural fears, imagining what Michael's approach might have been, I found a helpful guide for my own behavior, and I still call upon it whenever I find myself afraid. I imagine that you have a Michael in your life, too, whose example can be equally instructive and inspiring. And I bet you can think of a recent time when you wish you'd stood up for someone or something at work but instead convinced yourself that it wasn't in your best interests to do so. Researchers are demonstrating that the opposite may, in fact, be true. Where individuals speak up—keeping an organization true to its mission or defending peers—they have the ability to influence leadership and offer the hope for growth.

FIVE

Our Age of Anxiety

The central problem of our age is how to act decisively in the absence of certainty. —Bertrand Russell

As an entertainment television producer for more than twenty years, Catherine Mullally reveled in her high-stress job at MTV Networks. Cranky prima donna actors? Check. Tight budgets? Check. Impossible delivery schedules? Check. Too little sleep? Check. For her, it was the more stress the better. Spinning all those plates gave her energy, made her feel alive and connected to her work. It was *positive* stress.

So she was unprepared for the gut-wrenching anxiety she felt when she decided to launch her own consulting business in 2003. While she was a pro at dealing with her company's demanding schedules and budgets, she was unaccustomed to having uncertainty inextricably interwoven with her very identity—having decided to call her business the Catherine Mullally Communications Group. (And at the time she was starting her business, the "group" part of the name was, well, optimistic.) This entrepreneurial anxiety is common to many. Couple the basic kind of insecurity that anyone would feel when striking out on their own with the fact that she'd chosen to start her new business as her last child was entering college *and* as she was moving solo from the suburban family home where she and her children had lived into a small Manhattan apartment and one can see how she was dealing with both new levels and kinds of anxiety.

Her anxiety level: yellow.

Before she'd even had a chance to hang her shingle, Catherine was asked to deliver a keynote speech for Merrill Lynch's first annual Women's Symposium, both a blessing and a curse. "The audience was global, a hand-selected group of senior female financial advisors—all with high production records." Oh, and the venue? The ultraswanky midtown Manhattan Waldorf-Astoria Hotel ballroom, which seats 1,500. The debut for Catherine's business could not have been more high-profile. But her speech was also a singular opportunity to introduce her new business to a large pool of prospective clients, so she felt that it was well worth the risk.

But to make matters more stressful, the business climate at that moment in time was equally daunting. Merrill had been on the front pages of *The New York Times* business section for months as female executives from the firm waged a class-action suit. The women won that suit, and Merrill Lynch was required to not only pay out, but also to make fundamental shifts in its corporate culture. The annual symposium was the invention of then-CEO Stan O'Neal, and was conceptualized as a way to both create goodwill and kick-start visible programs for their senior women. "There had likely not been another time in the history of the firm when this particular audience was more geared up to hear something beyond rhetoric," said Catherine. "They were hungry and deserving of something new and useful. The more I learned about this engagement, the higher the stakes became."

Her new anxiety level: orange.

"Over the years," according to Catherine, she had "attended many events at the Waldorf, so I arrived" the day before her event "feeling like I knew the room." But she'd failed to take into consideration how having her face "magnified to the nth degree" on the twenty-five-foot video screens flanking the stage would intensify her sense of scrutiny, throwing not only every pore on her face but also the content of her speech into high relief. Learning that the event was also to be filmed and televised so that *everyone* who worked at Merrill could see it raised the bar for excellence even further in her mind.

Her latest anxiety level: red.

And if all of this pressure wasn't enough, finding out what she needed to know from the Merrill organizers also became challenging. The agenda was changing by the minute. The CEO was to attend as well as his senior executive team, and there were to be other keynotes. "At first I was to talk for an hour," said Catherine, "then forty-five minutes, then thirty-five minutes, then back to an hour again. Could I be there for meet and greet? Who knew?" It was difficult for Catherine to prepare, and the indecision augmented her already high degree of tension. Furthermore, in public speaking, there's a big difference between talking for thirty-five minutes versus sixty minutes. And finally, as Catherine said, "for an event to be meaningful, it's helpful to understand who is speaking in front of you and who will speak afterward." Names were bandied about, including Martha Stewart. But it took forever for the planners to settle on a final order. Finally, at the eleventh hour, the main keynote speaker was identified and booked—Anne Mulcahy, the chairman and then-CEO of Xerox, and a woman considered a "turn-around" expert. "At around this point," Catherine said, "I thought I was a good candidate for a turnaround. How did I end up here? Holy shit."

Her anxiety level now: Day-Glo hot pink?

"Needless to say, I was very nervous," said Catherine. "My new career was riding on this one event." She had delivered the same material, but not in a forty-five-minute format and only in smaller seminars and workshops. "In those days," she said, "I didn't trust the more intuitive process I rely on now. My reaction to the anxiety of this performance was *so* high. I was nerved up, made endless lists, and couldn't sleep. I literally memorized the entire talk. But I didn't really internalize the information–I just worked it to within an inch of its life. In retrospect, I see that this was the flawed way in which I'd dealt with anxiety for most of my life. I simply plowed through it like a dumb beast."

The anxiety had forced Catherine down a familiar road of preparation, yet still the unanticipated arose. "I forgot a line in the middle and my mind was a complete blank. Fortunately, I remembered that I could turn ever so slightly and see my slides—which contained mostly visual information—the perfect mnemonic for me."

When screening the tape later, Catherine realized that her moment of paralysis lasted only a second—and would not have been detected by the casual viewer. "This is what I tell my clients when helping them with public presentations," she now says. "It's a great stress-buster, and this hindsight was a good opportunity to take my own advice. Despite sleep deprivation and the insane amount of overpreparation, the event was a success."

Her final anxiety level: clear.

So what did Catherine learn? "Today, I have an entirely different relationship with anxiety and stress. I still have a healthy respect for [them] but no longer spend my time memorizing. I do continue to make lists. Mostly, I attend to anxiety from a more intuitive perspective." We'll never get rid of stress but we can be smarter about how to work with it. In Catherine's case, it was being thrust onto a stage and a public event. In other situations, it can mean the completion of a novel or the acceptance of a leadership position. As Catherine says, "I still find preparation invaluable, but have learned to trust that I will have exactly the information I need at the given moment. Anything that is missing will become clear in the doing."

WHAT IS ANXIETY?

For our earliest ancestors, anxiety was the early-warning system that preceded the immediate high-threat alert of specific, focused fear. The experience of anxiety is far more subtle and nuanced than the clanging *Danger! Danger!* feeling that flares up in our brains and nervous systems seconds before we step on a snake. The feeling of anxiety is fuzzier, less clearly focused than that of fear or anger, and is what we feel as we assess practically subconscious or barely conscious shifts in our environment that *might* indicate danger. A particular quality of stillness or quiet in the air, for instance, might simply be the tranquility brought about by animals relaxing in the shade of late-day heat, or nothing more worrisome than the approach of a thunderstorm—but it might also be a sign that a ferocious predator is lurking in the grasses or that a stampeding herd of wildebeest is about to thunder over the horizon. At work, the interminable stillness or quiet from a boss following a budget presentation could mean many things—that he's been positively inspired by the thoroughness of your analysis and is taking a moment to think through the issues you've identified before responding, or that's he's been stunned into silence by the inadequacy of your data. It may also simply be that he's tired and is taking a moment to gather his thoughts. It's the waiting, the not knowing what's going on in his mind, that is so anxiety-inducing. The *ambiguity* of not knowing how to interpret definitively that prickly back-of-the-neck, I-know-something-isn't-quite-right, is-the-other-shoe-going-to-drop? feeling is what we call anxiety.

Anxiety differs from other emotional states because it is often accompanied by *uncertainty.* With anxiety, there is rarely a single clear-cut course of action to be followed, which makes the anxious moment open to a wide range of speculation—and which can make it a chronic, debilitating state. Like every emotion, anxiety operates on three levels: what goes on in the brain, how we respond to those neural impulses, and our *subjective* experience of the situation. Should my family move into a cave to escape the storm or might it be safe enough to keep hunting? Should we stand motionless to avoid the predator, or slowly inch out of its field of vision? Should I take the promotion and move to Atlanta even though it means at least a year of commuting home on weekends? Should I ask for a raise after fourth quarter results or wait until my March performance evaluation? In the absence of definitive data, many decisions are literally nerve-racking.

On the neurological level, the physiological processes the brain goes through when we are anxious—the amygdala triggering the release of the stress hormones cortisol (to speed up the heart rate and dilate the pupils) and norepinephrine (to stimulate the release of glucose and help focus attention)—are roughly the same as what the brain exhibits when we are angry or afraid, different only in degree. But the level of uncertainty associated with anxiety is unique. We human animals have been bestowed with the ability to conjure practically limitless and distressing what-if scenarios to agonize over. While that ability to imagine and consider future scenarios is a critical life skill, overdoing it can defeat us. As Harvard professor of psychology Daniel Gilbert writes in *Stumbling on Happiness,* "What is the conceptual tie that binds *anxiety* and *planning*? Both of course are intimately connected to thinking about the future." Without some modicum of anxiety, people remain marooned in the here and now, incapable of envisioning the passage of time and potential consequences that cognitive psychologists say is the literally timeless way in which babies experience life. Planning, according to Gilbert, "requires that we peer into our futures, and anxiety is one of the reactions we may have when we do." We feel anxiety when we anticipate that something bad might happen, and, like Catherine, we plan by imagining how our actions will unfold over time.

Psychologist William James described his own battle with anxiety: "[It's] a horrible dread at the pit of my stomach . . . a sense of the insecurity of life." And unlike the emotions of anger or fear, which concentrate the mind and make a person take immediate corrective action to deal with the particular threat, with anxiety our interpretation of the situation may not suggest any specific action and may linger for longer periods of time.

Anxiety is a more diffuse emotion, more like fog versus the thunderbolts of fear or anger, and research has shown that anxiety also tends to be more closely associated with an individual's genetically determined predisposition. Eminent Harvard psychologist Jerome Kagan and his colleagues have examined temperament over decades in several longitudinal studies and concluded that some people are simply biologically inclined from birth to be more prone to arousal in the parts of their brains—the amygdala, the hypothalamus, and the hypothalamic-pituitary-adrenal axis, the circuitry controlling the stress hormone cortisol—that make us anxious. And those of us who tend to be anxious also have more activity in our right hemispheres, which is the half of the brain some research suggests is associated with anxiety and negative moods. It was such a relief to discover that I was probably *born* tense! Anxious people tend to be warier and more withdrawn, in contrast to those who are more willing to try new things and take risks. David Sloan Wilson of the State University of New York at Binghamton has studied inherited predispositions. And his studies have demonstrated that highly sensitive people behave consistently in a wide array of conditions. As he said in an interview in *The New York Times,* "sensitive people are 'exceptionally moved by symphonies,' and find graphic depictions of violence 'too hard to bear,' but they are also sensitive to drugs like caffeine, and their skin is easily irritated by the wrong soap, sunscreen, and fabric. Highly sensitive pigs squeal a lot; highly sensitive people feel a lot." As Wilson says, "Sure, it's painful at times. But just switch on some Bach and I'll squeal my thanks for thin skin." While it is clearly evolutionarily beneficial to have some members of the group be hypervigilant and hypersensitive to infinitesimal changes in their immediate environment (*do I smell smoke?*), it seems that these days more and more of us are anxious more of the time, and that is not such a good thing.

THE AGE OF ANXIETY

It was Marshall McLuhan, the author of the 1967 book *The Medium Is the Massage,* who identified a key factor driving our modern agitation: "Our age of anxiety is, in great part, the result of trying to do today's jobs with yesterday's tools." Nearly half a century later his words ring truer than ever. Our culture is chronically anxious precisely because we know that the acceleration of change in the world, from the technological to the biomedical to the environmental to the geopolitical, is outpacing our ability to deal. We can see the train barreling down the track toward us, but we don't know which way to jump. We are anxious, knowing that our habitual modes of thinking, our skills, and our jobs may be antiquated or even obsolete very much sooner than later.

It's no surprise that the National Institute of Mental Health has reported that anxiety is the most common mental illness in the United States. The NIMH estimates that forty million American adults, one in five of us, suffer acutely enough from the condition to be captured in their data. But what is less known is that anxiety and panic disorders are up to four times more common in women than in men in part because, as the neurobiologist Louann Brizendine writes, "women's brains activate more than men's in anticipation of fear or pain."

And those already vast numbers don't begin to reflect the millions of the rest of us more ordinarily anxious people who tough it out through sleepless nights and stressful days, fretting over ill-defined and often imaginary dangers beyond our control. Nearly half of the people (46 percent) in our Emotional Incidents in the Workplace Survey reported that they'd felt anxious at work during the past year, and that their stress accumulates from multiple sources and leaks out in myriad ways. And, as one might expect, the effect of stress in the workplace isn't limited *to* the workplace, as a similar proportion of workers (48 percent) said that the stress they experience in the workplace contaminates their home lives.

OPERATING IN THE PUBLIC EYE

In November 2009, an upbeat 62-year-old woman I'll call Jane Harris ran for reelection to the town board in a small town in upstate New York. A Democrat, she was opposed by a Republican who had never held public office and hadn't been particularly active in local organizations, but he was viewed as a reasonable guy with lots of friends.

"Everyone assured me," Jane says, "that I would have absolutely no trouble winning." But the special election in her Congressional district, which got huge national attention, changed everything. The supporters of the conservative candidate—who had driven the "too liberal" Republican nominee to drop out of the race and endorse the Democrat—mobilized thousands of very conservative voters. With the change in fervor during the campaign season, Jane became more and more anxious, but it wasn't until Election Day that she realized how precarious her situation was.

Her first clue that it was going to be a bad day was early in the morning, when one of the poll watchers reported that "busloads" of people from a conservative evangelical church were being brought to the polls. In the evening, Jane and her supporters gathered at the local inn to wait for the returns. "There were reporters and photographers there," she said, "so I felt like any reaction or emotion on my part was being played out on a public stage. At 9:30 or so we began to get phone calls from people at the polling places."

Like Catherine Mullally, Jane had a lot of her identity riding on this election and, like Catherine, her high anxiety was playing out on a very public stage—in front of her peers, her supporters, her rivals, and her whole community.

"There are six districts in the town, and I lost the first one," Jane says, "which wasn't surprising, since it was a strong Republican area. But then I got a call from the district where we had done very well in 2005 and, unbelievably, I lost that district, too. I was an absolute wreck at this point. I was horribly anxious about the outcome, but felt I had to continue looking optimistic for everyone else." Jane worried that she had let down all her friends who had given money and time, and felt that she had been stupid to assume that the election wouldn't really be contested. "In the end, I won," she says, "but the results weren't final until the next morning, and suffice it to say that I did not sleep well that night."

SECOND-GUESSING YOURSELF

A 35-year-old woman I'll call Sarah Smith, a global home video marketing director based in Los Angeles, is the sort of kind and sharing person anyone would want as a friend, but also the sort who worries a lot about what others think of her. Not long after she and her husband moved to Los Angeles a few years ago, her mother, who was visiting, suggested that she pick some of the lemons from the tree in their backyard and take them to the office. "I thought it was a cute idea when mom bagged the lemons. But then I started having second thoughts—would I be bringing too much of my personality into the office, was it unprofessional?" Sarah was new to her job, trying to fit into a new team and demonstrate competence and authority, but worried about standing out.

"I went ahead and did it," she says, "even writing a little note in yellow and green with an illustration of a tiny lemon tree I'd found on the Internet saying, 'These were picked by Max, aged three, and he hopes you enjoy them this weekend.' That's me and just the way I am. All of the junior people were incredibly nice and thanked me. And not a single one of the senior people said a word. They walked right by, and I felt uncomfortable. Was this not the kind of place where people did 'nice' things like that? And I worried that maybe in the future I'd better not put myself out there that way."

Should Sarah have taken the lemons to work? Could anything be *less* of a big deal? Yet for Sarah, the incident in one bold stroke seemed to illustrate the cultural norms of her new office, that for executives work was work and home was home. No doubt Sarah had been aware beforehand, subconsciously, of how her peers would view her gifted lemons—hence her anxiety. Yet if you *always* allow your gut to rule when you are anxious about something at work, you may lose opportunities to communicate or achieve something new. It's easy to imagine that Sarah's colleagues could have found her gesture charming and authentic—a clear signal of her accessibility and warmth. In either case, a very modest gesture was blown out of proportion in Sarah's mind.

THE EMPEROR'S NEW CLOTHES

Many of the people I interviewed confessed to feeling a personally corrosive emperor's-new-clothes sort of professional anxiety—the kind that has nothing to do with the objective or measurable aspects of business and everything to do with their *internal* sense of self-esteem. In the classic Andersen fairy tale, two weavers dupe the emperor, telling him that the fabulous new suit they've woven for him is invisible to those not worthy to see. When the king passes before his subjects, a child in the crowd points out his obvious nakedness, but the emperor carries on as if he were clothed. When we describe ourselves as feeling like the emperor at work we are primarily confessing to feeling fraudulent, perhaps having oversold ourselves by projecting a false or misconstrued competency in areas beyond our skill set, which, in turn, causes us to feel constantly anxious, fearing exposure of our failings by colleagues. So many of us live with this kind of anxiety of being unmasked that the phenomenon has a name: the imposter syndrome. According to Georgia State University psychology professor emerita Pauline Rose Clance and psychologist Suzanne Imes, the researchers who first identified this emotional state, imposters attribute their success to luck rather than to their own abilities. Yet this sort of anxiety is complicated because there is a thin line between anxiety that enervates, undermining our ability to accomplish anything, and the sort that motivates, inspiring us to rise to new challenges. Were we never to take risks, reach a bit beyond our comfortable grasp, we'd never suffer from the syndrome—and we'd also never grow.

I have never had any specific training for any position I've ever had, so it goes without saying that at the start of every job I've been anxious that others would discover that I was an imposter. Twenty-four years ago my husband and two friends started *Spy,* an independent satirical magazine. While my husband and his editorial partner in the venture had both been writers, the partner was new to this country, my husband hadn't been an editor, and their third partner, although an MBA experienced in venture capital, had never run a business. Nevertheless, they secured seed money and launched the magazine in October 1986. They had hired experienced salespeople to sell advertising space, believing, not irrationally, that professionals in that revenue-generating area would compensate for the founders' lack of expertise in that aspect of the enterprise. But in reality the professionals, who in their previous jobs were accustomed to selling editorial content that promoted specific products like cosmetics and fashion, were unable to figure out how to sell *Spy*'s quirky and unusual content.

So I came aboard to help. I had sold television programming for the Children's Television Workshop, so I assumed that I could sell magazine advertising. How different could it be? Guess what? Dramatically. On my first few sales calls I blustered through meetings, slinging CPMs (cost per thousand readers) and rate bases around as if I knew what I was talking about. But I rapidly realized that I was in way over my head and that bravado alone wasn't enough to convince advertisers to part with their money. I discovered two things that did help. First, I started telling people the moment I went into a call that I was a novice in the field, but that I was a novice because I was passionate about what my husband and now I were trying to do. I knew every single word in the magazine, knew why the pieces had been assigned and how they had been produced. So I explained this. The second thing I did was to say, "I know this magazine is right for your product, but I need your help in understanding what you need from us to help you take this leap."

From the moment I began to tell people that I was new to a job that deeply mattered to me and asked for help, I *got* it and we began to do gangbuster business. And my anxiety evaporated. As a result, through sheer necessity, I happened on one of the most effective ways to deal with the kind of imposter anxiety we experience when trying new things far beyond our usual skill set. Just admit when you don't know something. Ask questions. It's that simple. Now I never try to bluff my way through anything important that I really don't understand. It's an effective strategy, and I encourage you to try it.

WHY BEING HONEST ABOUT ANXIETY CAN BE GOOD FOR YOU AND GOOD FOR BUSINESS

I was curious to know if chronic anxiety and amped-up stress levels compromised our general effectiveness. For help in understanding what biochemical effect anxiety might have on work performance, I turned to Daniela Schiller, a PhD in neuropsychology and a postdoctoral researcher at the Center for Neural Science and Psychology at New York University. Schiller, a warm and engaging 37-year-old, investigates the neural mechanisms that underlie emotion control. She focuses on understanding emotion before the fact, from the chemical precursors to the expression of an emotion, while I was more interested in what happens after the fact, from the moment of experience through the practical consequence of its expression. As a caveat before we started to talk, Schiller explained that she was not an expert in all the areas in which I had questions, but that she would offer her opinion when she felt that she had something of value to contribute. She also qualified her responses by saying that the nature of her research was circumscribed by laboratory conditions, with studies carefully sequenced to build provable conclusions—in other words, the scientific experimental method. The messy, multifaceted aspects of the real workplace wouldn't offer quick or definitive assessments.

We began by exploring how problematic workplace anxiety is

for people. When a person is under chronic stress, Schiller explained, the structure of neurons can be altered. Neurons have bodies and branches used to communicate with other cells, and the more branches the neurons have, the better the communication. Chronic stress causes a person to experience a loss of higher brain control over emotion—in old-fashioned Freudian terms, the superego succumbs to the id. Stress *reduces* the number of branches in the prefrontal cortex, a regulatory part of the brain connected to memory and depression, which in turn causes dendrites, the branches that relay information between neurons, to shrink. Another region vulnerable to this effect is the hippocampus, a part of the brain exercising "contextual" control over emotions, that is, the expression of learned emotional responses in the appropriate interpersonal contexts. Reduced prefrontal and hippocampal activity may deplete normal levels of emotion inhibition and appropriate expression.

I asked Schiller what we could do to counterbalance the negative effects of anxiety. "Well, I would say just avoid chronic stress, or attempt to have relief from prolonged stress." The good news, she added, is that "there is evidence for reversal of these effects—a rebranching, if you will."

What Schiller was referring to is new research that indicates that our brains actually have the ability to stimulate new neuron growth, and to increase our "neuroplasticity"—the notion that the brain, even in adults, continues to change in response to experiences and perceptions. We now know that our brains are not objects fixed forever in late adolescence, but rather, like other parts of our body that continue to change during our lifetime, they respond and even *grow* in response to the ways in which we use them.

This idea that we do not have to persist in a perpetual state of anxiety but instead have the ability to change the way our mind is working is radical and refreshing. As with exercising only one group of muscles in our bodies, if we excessively favor one side of our emotional lives, in this instance the anxiety-inducing side, we'll develop psychological and behavioral limps, shuffles, and stoops. Everyone knows not to work your triceps without also working your biceps, your lats without your delts, or your quads without your hamstrings. We get the physical analogy—so why is it hard to appreciate that we can work our emotional "muscles" in an analogous way? If we focus *only* on negative experiences, fretting and worrying over every slight, our emotional resiliency muscles atrophy.

THE POWER OF POSITIVE THINKING

Historically, psychopathology—mental illness and its underlying causes and treatment protocols—was a primary focus of research. A new movement, positive psychology, encourages people to pay attention to and develop a group of core "virtues"—courage, wisdom, humanity, justice, temperance, and transcendence—that can help our lives go *right.* This is a key insight driving the positive psychology movement, pioneered over the last decade or so by Martin Seligman, director of the University of Pennsylvania's Positive Psychology Center and author of *Authentic Happiness,* and Daniel Gilbert, a Harvard psychology professor and author of *Stumbling on Happiness.* And while "the power of positive thinking" is derided as a corny, conservative artifact of 1950s Americana, as was the suggestion that we "accentuate the positive and eliminate the negative" considered just a chirpy 1944 song lyric, maybe Norman Vincent Peale and Johnny Mercer were on to something.

Central to the emerging discipline is the notion that the pursuit and development of these virtues is not the exclusive province of Eastern mystics or "spiritual" enthusiasts, but rather something accessible by virtually all of us, even the most secular and skeptical. It's liberating to think that by taking time to register and enjoy aspects of everyday life that delight—the moment of hope sparked by teaching kids to read, the inspiration found in a team working seamlessly together, the beauty of sunlight streaming through a red maple leaf—we may be encouraging new kinds of neuron growth and increasing our neuroplasticity.

Just as research has demonstrated that the portions of the brain that control motor coordination are *physically larger* in violinists or professional baseball players and those parts of the brain that control recognition and memory tasks are physically larger in chess players, so it seems that devoting more of our mental firepower toward the life-enhancing activities in our lives might strengthen the parts of our brains cued to their appreciation.

Regularly diverting our attention from the irritating, nitpicking small things in life toward expansive, inspiration-generating potential in the world also improves what psychologists call the "recovery function," which is the time it takes a person to return to a baseline condition of calm after being upset. And this has demonstrable, long-term physical health benefits, as noted by Daniel Goleman in his book *Destructive Emotions:* "The person who is able to recover quickly also has a lower level of cortisol." As I've described, cortisol plays a key role in stress—high levels have been linked to post-traumatic stress disorder and depression. Ergo, the better one is able to control stress, the better one's health and mood.

It also appears that stress affects our creativity. By studying people's "Aha!" moments of insight, Northwestern University psychologist Mark Jung-Beeman found that one's brain state before addressing a problem can importantly influence the creativity of one's proposed solution. He discovered that if someone is too focused, too wound up, the scope of their problem solving is reduced. "If you're in an environment that forces you to produce and produce and you feel very stressed," he told *The New Yorker,* "then you're not going to have any insights."

"There's a good reason Google puts Ping-Pong tables in its headquarters," writes John Kounios, a cognitive neuroscientist at Drexel University who partnered with Jung-Beeman in his research. "If you want to encourage insights, then you've got to also encourage people to relax." Their research has found that on average, people in good moods solve 20 percent more word association puzzles than a control group given the same amount of time. Is 20 percent not rational and quantitative and bottom-line enough to convince managers that smart emotional management isn't a touchy-feely waste of time?

BUILDING YOUR ANXIETY EMOTION MANAGEMENT TOOLKIT

Unlike the more specifically provoked emotions such as anger—*She didn't promote me, He stole credit for my work*—anxiety is often a free-floating condition that exists over time. And while anxiety may be fed by real, external factors—the economy is bad, our industry is in trouble—it is nearly always kept under control or turned destructive by how we choose to process it internally. When we fret, especially when it becomes irrational or compulsive, we fan the hot coal bed of anxiety until it bursts into flames. And so it follows that anxiety must be *remedied* over time as well, by learning to fret less. The strategies that follow offer a range of ways to minimize anxiety.

EMT—JUST SAY "OHM" OR JUST GET MOVING

An Asian practice—meditation in its various forms—is one relaxation technique under study as a means of reducing anxiety. And the data are encouraging. As one example, a study in the department of physiology at Chlalongkom University in Bangkok of fifty-two men practicing Buddhist meditation found that cortisol levels, blood pressure levels, and pulse rate were all significantly reduced after meditation.

Reducing anxiety may have even farther-reaching benefits for women. Cardiovascular disease, which has been clinically correlated with high stress and anxiety levels, is the number one killer of women in the United States, accounting for 26 percent of deaths and killing more American women then all cancers combined, according to the Centers for Disease Control. Yet because it is only within the last decade that scientists have begun to realize the extent to which women's biochemical and hormonal constitution may influence their predisposition toward contracting a variety of diseases, there is no clear consensus regarding specific benefits of stress-reduction protocols for women.

Until that consensus emerges, for those of us who feel anxious a lot of the time and for whom the idea of sitting down to meditate is a foreign concept, I have found several other practical, physical ways to help me slow my overactive, anxiety-prone mind. Every day I try to walk a mile outdoors. The methodical rhythm is soothing, and hearing birds chirp, watching dogs frisk, and observing other people going about their business instantly decompresses me. It's almost miraculous how quickly my tension diminishes. And on days when I have a bit more time, I try to fit in a yoga session or tai chi class. Moving in unison with a group of like-minded people for a sustained period of time, fully focused on breath and ritualized movements, serves as a powerful antidote to anxiety.

EMT—SMELL THE ROSES

I've stolen an elegant practice from Japanese culture that helps me step outside anxiety at work. Many Japanese have a small, recessed area, or *tokonoma,* in their houses where they place objects of singular beauty or personally meaningful artistic value—

a piece of calligraphy, a bonsai tree, a flower arrangement—for contemplation. The area is a sanctuary, celebrating artistic endeavor or natural splendor, and serves to connect one to the more spiritual or meaningful aspects of life. When passing a *tokonoma* it is common to take a moment to pause for reflection.

At work, one need not follow this practice literally—most of us don't work in environments that lend themselves to something as precious-seeming as this. But it is very easy to establish a modest equivalent anywhere—a desk drawer, on your interior cubicle wall, in your briefcase or pocketbook. I suggest having the object near you at all times, creating your own always accessible *tokonoma*. It can be anything that lifts your spirits and draws you outside the feedback loop in your head—a particularly cheerful drawing your kid made, a glittering rock you picked up on your last vacation, a postcard of Monet's *Water Lilies*—whatever object best calms and inspires you. When you feel anxiety gaining the upper hand—before you head into a big meeting, after a confrontation with a boss—take a moment to plant your feet firmly on the ground, close your eyes, take five deep breaths, and then open your eyes and gaze at the object. Fresh observation should change your perspective and lift your mood.

EMT—WHAT'S THE WORST THAT CAN HAPPEN?

When I prodded Jane Harris to reveal how she managed to maintain her outward calm while waiting for the returns on election night, she paused a moment. "I think having a good sense of humor was essential, and the wine helped," she said, "but really it was two key strategies—although I'm reluctant to use that word because they were not wholly conscious at the time. First, to try to look at the situation from the *outside*—what were the issues surrounding the vote that were unique [and] that might have shaped the results in ways beyond my or the party's control? And then I tried to look at it from a very *personal* perspective: what would the worst-case outcome be? Well, when I looked at it like that, I realized it wasn't so bad, since if I'd lost it would have been a huge weight off my shoulders and I'd have had more free time." By pushing yourself to contemplate personal Armageddon, it's possible to step back and realize that the worst as envisioned in that moment is often or usually not so terrible.

EMT—DIAGRAM WHAT YOU NEED TO DO

One approach to changing our relationship with anxiety is to channel the excess energy produced by our agitation from a ruminative state into something productive. Instead of simply *worrying,* for instance, about the upcoming meeting, sit down, like Catherine Mullally, and write your presentation. Then get up and rehearse it. By breaking your anxiety into discrete, easily accomplished tasks and redirecting your tension into action, you can turn your emotional state to your advantage. In fact, one in six people in our Emotional Incidents in the Workplace Survey reported that they believed that stress helped them perform better at work. I'm betting that it's because most of them have taught themselves to use it rather than be undone by it.

SIX

Empathy: We *Do* Get by with a Little Help from Our Friends

One can overcome the forces of negative emotions, like anger and hatred, by cultivating their counterforces, like love and compassion. —the Dalai Lama

Dickie Davis, who as the director of terminal operations and customer service runs much of Miami International Airport day to day, comes across as the quintessential female executive: tailored suits, classic understated accessories (pearls and a tank watch), conservative horn-rimmed glasses, and a Meg-Ryan's-older-sister look. At 59, she is amazingly a thirty-seven-year veteran of MIA. But her job comes with stress levels that most managers seldom experience: she oversees a 106-member team that speaks nine different languages, and she is responsible for the safekeeping of thirty-four million passengers a year, the 90,000 (as it happens, mostly foreign) people passing each day through the third-largest international airport in the United States. Her bailiwick includes seventy-one airlines spread over seven million square feet of interior space—the equivalent of 122 football fields containing 177 escalators, 64 power walks, 302 restrooms, and 180 concessionaires. You would think that the sheer frenzied volume of moving parts in her job, the scale of the enterprise, and the stakes involved would eliminate any possibility for personal attention, or worrying much about individual feelings. You would be mistaken.

Dealing with so many and such a wide range of people is indeed, she says, "tough, tough, tough." But having spent several days shadowing her on the job, I witnessed firsthand the priority she places on managing people's *emotions.* "If you are at my door and are having a fit because your luggage got lost or your daughter passed out and had to be taken to the hospital, we don't want you to say you hate the city of Miami because this happened at MIA and no one was nice to you. That's what terminal ops is all about."

Dickie credits her success at the job to a high emotional intelligence, or EQ, a hyper-intuitive ability to figure out what is important to her bosses, her customers, and her employees. She says the one thing that "really makes me insane is personal injustice, people mistreating others. I have no tolerance for people mistreating others, especially those who can't always fight for themselves." Kindness and a fundamentally emotional devotion to service are what drive her. "It's my passion that differentiates me and my team from others. If someone just shows up and suits up, 'just does the work,' then I don't want them on my team.

"I was extremely lucky to find a job with a mission that is ideally suited to my personality," Dickie says. "When I first started working [here] in 1973, there was no woman of any kind in management. Everyone I worked with was ex-military pilots whose attitude was just, 'Goddamn it, *do* this,' and that almost iconic [command-and-control] behavior taught me that I wanted to manage differently. I wanted to work from my strength, which is empathy."

And Dickie really walks the walk. Twelve years ago, airport management participated in a metropolitan "Boss-for-a-Day" program in which kids from underprivileged, inner-city schools teamed up with "mentors" and shadowed them for a day at work. Dickie's assigned kid, David, was a 16-year-old recent immigrant from Jamaica. "Something about this boy was very different, very special. I could see how bright he was and how he hung on every word I said and took the entire experience in. Something about him really touched me, and as he left that day I gave him a book about the history of blacks in aviation, and told him to call me if he ever wanted a job. Well, not three weeks later he took me up on my offer. But during the call and from that day at the airport, I realized that he might have some sort of learning disability—the way he spoke and put his words together wasn't always easy to understand. But somehow I was on his frequency—I understood everything he said."

David enrolled in an airport internship program. "And I came to realize that this kid, going into his junior year of high school, could barely read. I went home that night and sobbed. And that was a turning point for me. I was outraged by the injustice. As a child I'd had serious scoliosis, which had given me an acute sense of otherness, and in David I saw the same wounded child that I had been." From that day forward, Dickie became David's champion. "We all have character traits, positive and negative, and one of my positives is that I'm fiercely protective of people who are at a disadvantage." She tutored him in reading, found professionals who identified his specific learning disabilities, helped him graduate high school, and found him funding for college. David worked at the airport thirty hours a week during high school, building up to a full-time load while also attending college.

David, now a college graduate, works in Dickie's terminal operations division. One day not long ago, he said in passing, "God has put you in my life. You are my angel. Do you think I will ever have the chance to be an angel to someone?" Shortly thereafter, the two of them were walking together through the teeming terminal when, out of the corner of his eye, he happened to see a woman forty feet away collapse to the floor crying. "He's just so intuitive," Dickie says, "and he keyed right in on this woman I hadn't even seen, and he ran over, took her in his arms, and said, 'You're going to be okay, I'm right here.' I looked at David and said, 'Now *you're* the angel.' "

WHAT IS COMPASSION?

What motivates people like Dickie to fight for those less fortunate than they? Empathy and compassion.

Compared to the big "negative" emotions—anger, fear, anxiety—compassion and its cousin, empathy, fulfill a very different but nonetheless essential human evolutionary function. As I've said, anger and fear originate in the more primal part of our brain and tend to arise in response to a threat to the well-being of an individual, whereas compassion and empathy arise more from a desire to ensure the survival of the species. Fear and anxiety are about avoiding harm; anger is about deterring or punishing the harm-doer; empathy and compassion are about mitigating the pain of those who have been harmed, especially those outside one's closest circle. And all have been essential to human survival.

Empathy is the general capacity we developed to imagine and share the feelings of others, while the closely related compassion is its "applied" version, directly linked to the pain of others, and the instinctive wish to alleviate suffering. It's fighting fire with honey, using positive emotion to moderate negative emotion: empathy and compassion can act as balms for others in the grip of fear and anger—particularly in the workplace, when they've been triggered by psychological rather than physical blows. Our ability to envision another person's anxiety about making a huge presentation and thus offer them encouragement or support, for instance, may serve to boost their confidence while simultaneously curbing our potential impatience with what we might see as their perhaps less-than-professional behavior. Empathy at work can promote a level of altruism that inspires us to stay late helping a young colleague make a breakthrough on a project or to take on an additional workload to help a colleague with a sick child. Or it can be integral to the job itself, as with Dickie, motivating her to make sure that every person who passes through (or works at) the Miami airport is treated with respect.

While the pathways for all emotions overlap, those for empathy and compassion relate mostly to the neocortex or cognitive areas of our brains. The hormone oxytocin, discussed in Chapter Two, fosters social bonding. And because the female pituitary gland secretes more oxytocin than the male pituitary gland, among other reasons including social reinforcement, women tend to be more attentive to emotional nuance in other people. Interestingly, while women produce great quantities of oxytocin immediately following the birth of their children, men, somewhat surprisingly, also do—nature's way of ensuring that both parents are motivated to protect their offspring.

Additionally, some neuroscience research has suggested the existence of what have been termed "mirror neurons," which activate in our brains as we observe (or even imagine) behavior in others, automatically arousing similar brain patterns in the observer. As society became more and more complex over the eons, this behavioral mirroring may have extended our empathic range beyond our kin to serve larger societal and cultural needs. So when Bill Clinton suggested that he could "feel your pain," he was, in neurological terms, declaring a basic human truth.

The workplace is far and away the most complicated social terrain in which we regularly operate. All of the individual aspects of our identity—gender, class, race, education, competence, and power—are in constant interaction with those of everyone else with whom we work. The imperative to try to understand others' points of view—to be empathetic—is plainly important in any collaborative endeavor. And the results from our Emotional Incidents in the Workplace survey reflect this larger social drive to relate to our fellow workers. Almost 80 percent of the women and 69 percent of the men in our survey believe that when people show emotion in the workplace, it makes them seem more human, more approachable—that is, it provokes their colleagues to feel empathy. Furthermore, 93 percent of the women and 83 percent of the men said that being sensitive to others' emotions at work is an asset.

WHY EMPATHY IS IMPORTANT

Before he nominated Sonia Sotomayor to the Supreme Court, President Obama said that "empathy" is "an essential ingredient for arriving at just decisions and outcomes," and that in choosing a nominee he wanted someone "who understands that justice isn't about some abstract legal theory." When Sotomayor's opponents turned "empathy" into a negative catchword, which they claimed meant the unjudicial imposition of liberal legal outcomes, David Brooks, the conservative op-ed columnist for *The New York Times,* called foul: "It is incoherent to say that a judge should base an opinion on reason and not emotion because emotions are an inherent part of decision-making. Emotions are the processes we use to assign value to different possibilities. . . . People without social emotions like empathy are not objective decision-makers." Politics notwithstanding, this public discourse about the need for empathy to be viewed as an essential asset in the workplace was important.

Because not only are emotions like empathy important to

decision-making, it turns out that they impact the bottom line as well. For instance, a 1996 study published in *Training and Development* that assessed the value of training workers at a manufacturing plant in emotional management skills found that filings for union grievances were reduced by two-thirds and productivity goals increased by $250,000. Organizations that explicitly incorporate empathy coaching in how to treat customers and clients—that train employees to focus on how their work *affects others* rather than simply on getting the job done—have reported higher rates of job satisfaction and productivity. And a study of a Fortune 400 health insurance company conducted by Peter Salovey, another founder of the emotional intelligence movement and a psychology professor at Yale, looked at the correlation between emotional intelligence and salary, and determined that those participants who were rated highest by their peers in emotional intelligence received the biggest raises and were promoted most frequently.

Empathy can even be a nontraditional resource for identifying new business opportunities. "The exec team had coaches assigned to us who conducted 360-degree reviews," says Ann Sarnoff, chief operating officer of BBC Worldwide America, "and it turned out that I was off-the-chart empathetic. My first thought was 'Damn, why do I have to be so *feeling*?' But my coach said I could turn that characteristic into strength and use my empathy to better understand our customers. Since then, I've focused that empathy into an intense interest in the end user, which has helped me develop new business ideas and marketing."

THE VALUE OF SPEAKING FROM THE HEART

Dr. Kerry Sulkowicz, a psychiatrist and management consultant for the Boswell Group, suggests that "when a leader or executive has a spontaneous display of emotion, like crying or showing sadness, it can have a very *positive* effect on an organization, by revealing his or her core human attribute of empathy. The *authenticity* of the response can lend increased credibility to subsequent actions on the part of the executive." In *Speaking from the Heart,* Pennsylvania State University psychologist Stephanie Shields writes that "a person who 'speaks from the heart' is far more credible than someone who merely speaks. And because the consensus is that women tend to be the more emotionally accessible gender, when men empathetically connect on the job, it tends to be even more highly prized."

Jeff Dunn, the 54-year-old chairman of HIT Entertainment, a preschool media company, appears to be a stereotypically buttoned-up, buttoned-down, hyperrational guy. Yet his management style belies this impression: "I'm always trying to tell a story or paint a picture," he says, "and I believe that people are emotional human beings and to reach [employees] you have to connect with them emotionally. I'm looking to understand who these people are, to get the best out of them, and so my experience has been that to really maximize performance you have to know what makes people tick. I've cried in my office, more than once," he says, "and not always behind a closed door. The last time was about a year ago, when I had to lay off a bunch of people, and I went to the staff and I said, 'I told you when I took this job that I'd do everything I can, but I can no longer carry all of you.' It was a very emotional moment, but the feedback I got after the meeting was astounding—people came to thank me for my honesty and I think they knew my emotion was authentic."

Jeff took personal responsibility for the tough decision, and his tears lent emotional credence to the truthfulness of his message and reinforced trust in his leadership among his employees. In *Emotions in the Workplace,* sociologist and management consultant Willem Mastenbroek says that the rules within contemporary organizations are in flux and that leaders today bolster their position of power the more honestly they allow their personality to shine, "for only if you are comfortable will you be able to put other persons at ease and in the end, that's what it is all about." When Jeff chose to reveal his distress, he was empathetic, allowing the feelings of his employees—anxious, nervous, concerned, scared—to be validated.

Like 9 percent of the men in our survey, Herb Scannell, the president of BBC Worldwide America, found times when the lines between his private and professional lives were blurred, when his love for his work and for his family mutually reinforced each other. He clearly remembers giving a speech about empowerment for girls at a Girls Inc. awards ceremony during a time of inordinate work pressure at Nickelodeon, where he worked at the time. "I had just recently put my mom, who has Alzheimer's, in a nursing home," he said, "and the young girl to whom I was giving the award had the unusual name of Zulma, the name of my mom's oldest sister." During the speech, the combination of the theme of empowering girls, the recent birth of his daughter, his pride in Nickelodeon, and thoughts about his mom added up to an unexpectedly emotional moment for him. "I found myself starting to tear up." And he got a standing ovation.

NOT SPEAKING FROM THE HEART

Of course there are times when ego compounded by thoughtlessness squelches empathy. One personally painful example cropped up as I interviewed others with whom I'd worked while at Nickelodeon. I was stunned when Scott Davis, who had been the executive vice president for recreation, told me that I'd once made *him* cry. After I had become the worldwide creative director for the company, Scott was overseeing the creation of a Nickelodeon mini–theme park at Shea Stadium in New York City. To my mind Scott was a hardware guy with no experience managing creative execution or overseeing brand who had come out of operations to run Nick Studios. When at one of our monthly off-site strategy meetings he presented the graphics that had been designed for the facility, I shot him down, explaining in no uncertain terms why I felt the work was subpar. At a subsequent meeting with our boss, Gerry, he told me, he'd cried while seeking her help because he felt that I'd attacked his work without having actually examined it thoroughly. "I felt Gerry hadn't defined our roles clearly enough, and all of a sudden here come all of these creative rules," he said. "To me it felt like it came from left field." As Scott spoke I recalled the incident, and while I continue to believe that the work he presented was inferior to our usual standards, I felt horrible. I'm pretty sure that at best I'd been dismissive of the work done by Scott's team and at worst condescending to him personally during my appraisal. By not putting myself in his shoes and imagining how vulnerable he might have felt, particularly as a tech guy presenting creative materials to a group of executives who led the creative units of the company, I had unnecessarily hurt a good guy's feelings. And for what? To support my subjective notion of what Nickelodeon's merchandise should look like at a baseball park? To boost my standing among my peers by taking Scott down a notch? It is not a moment of which I am proud. In hindsight the cost of my sharp criticism outweighed the benefit, and I bet that if I'd taken a less confrontational tone I would have been able to nurture a more successful working relationship with Scott. It was my loss and if I could have a "do-over," I would take it.

A far more extreme example of anti-empathy haunted a senior female ad executive who worked for a woman who was terribly inconsistent, saying one thing one minute and changing her mind the next. It made her an extremely difficult boss. One of the ad exec's colleagues was a nice, sweet guy, "not the typical up-and-coming ambitious career guy," she said. One day their boss lashed out and was inappropriately harsh with the man. "I happened to be there," she said, "and he started to well up and cry, so he went into his office." And that would have been that, except that the boss didn't keep the moment to herself. She used the incident, *naming* the guy, in discussions with other senior managers to illustrate just how tough a manager she was, and how pathetic a guy he was. "It was this titillating kind of thing," the ad exec explained, "where the people she told the story to responded with a little bit of 'I can't believe he did that!' and a little bit of 'Aren't you tough!' that gave her just enough juice to be emotionally rewarded for her behavior." And it gave them just enough prurient rubbernecking to be grateful that they had escaped her wrath. At the end of the day, the boss was a brilliant woman but just a hideous manager, and every one of the ten people who reported directly to her ultimately quit—which in turn resulted in her own ousting. The woman's lack of empathy was toxic to everyone who worked for her and finally to herself.

WHERE THE RUBBER HITS THE ROAD

The one time at work when compassion should be *obligatory* is when people are fired. But alas, that is all too often not the case. Over the course of my research I interviewed many people about their experiences being fired or firing someone. And while it seems almost too obvious to mention, a senior female Hollywood talent agent, whom I'll call Martha Jones, offered one of the best strategies for what is inevitably a miserable conversation. "I say right out front that this is not going to be a good conversation, and I think by being direct, it makes it easier for them to listen and they can move past the drama of anticipation."

This is precisely what the male editor who fired Walter Kirn did not do. Martha has observed that when men fire people they have a tendency to want to control the situation by saying something like, "You shouldn't feel so bad because of blah, blah, blah." She, on the other hand, is very careful *not* to tell a person that they should feel a certain way. From Martha's perspective, men want to make the moment more comfortable, whereas she says that, "I feel like I'm able to be okay with silence and with the person crying. I don't want to rush them through it and don't want them to feel mortified that they've let down the ultimate wall. Depending on how well I know them I might rub their back to comfort them—or at the minimum I'll say, 'I'll let you cry for a minute.' " Martha's experience has taught her that the more comfortable we can be with the uncomfortableness of the situation, the better. And specifically, "if you allow the person a little time to pull him- or herself together, and offer them a Kleenex, then you can get back to the more relevant questions. In fact, there actually have been a couple of people over the years who I wish *would* have started crying, because I think it would have been a healthier release than going immediately to anger."

Jim Kelly, the top editor of *Time* from 2001 to 2006, has similar advice. As the print magazine publishing model started becoming untenable, he was responsible for overseeing the first of several rounds of major layoffs. "Ever since 1986, when I laid off a colleague for the first time, I've had a box of Kleenex on my desk because that first time I had nothing to offer her when she started to cry, other than those coarse paper hand towels from the bathroom. It was a miserable experience to watch those little cardboardy pieces begin to stick to her face, and I never wanted anyone to ever have to endure that kind of experience again."

FROM BAD TO WORSE

Let's take a look at what happened to a successful book publisher whom I'll call Rachel Knox who was fired from her previous job a few years ago.

"I did not deserve to be fired," Rachel said. She and her boss had had a real power struggle, but over a lunch she thought they'd resolved it. So when—in what she now sees as "a chicken-shit way"—her boss sent her an e-mail on the Friday after that lunch asking her to come in on Monday at 9 a.m. to talk about bonuses and "other good things," she felt completely sandbagged when instead of talking about "other good things," he fired her. "The way he did it was so meandering that at first I honestly didn't know what he was talking about," she said.

"Once I figured out that he was firing me, I burst into tears—but they were tears of rage." Rachel understood firsthand what psychologist Carol Tavris described in *Anger: The Misunderstood Emotion*—that women often cry at work when they wish they could get angry (see Chapter Three). Finally Rachel said, " 'I need some Kleenex,' and he said, 'but I don't have any.' " And she said, "Who fires people without having a box of Kleenex in their office? I've fired people, and had both men and women cry, and I have one rule—No performance conversation without a box of Kleenex!"

Rachel thinks that the fact that she cried made her seem inferior in his mind, as if she deserved to be fired. She couldn't stop crying. "The political battle was such and the anger was such that I had to go into another room in the office, still without Kleenex. I called my best friend and she said to me, 'Do you have sunglasses?' I said, 'No, it's January.' " Her friend showed up ten minutes later and because Rachel wasn't allowed back to her office while Human Resources was telling her staff the news, her buddy collected her coat and bag from her office and handed her "the biggest pair of Jackie O. sunglasses you've ever seen. I put them on and we just swept out of the building. And that was my first step in regaining my calm."

Compassion is the keen awareness of the interdependence of all things. —Thomas Merton

There will come a time for all of us when what's happening in our lives *outside* of work will seep in and bring low even the most determinedly cheerful of us. And if each of us starts every day with the presumption that at least one person with whom we work will be feeling under the weather or have a sick child or straying spouse or ailing parent, then we can bring to work the mind-set of "do unto others emotionally as you'd have them do unto you."

The whole time I'd been negotiating that Sony video deal for Nickelodeon, my father had been fighting a losing battle against multiple myeloma, an extremely painful and at that time usually fatal bone marrow cancer. I'd been shuttling between New York City and the hospital in Hilton Head, South Carolina, where my father had traveled from Kansas City for treatment by an oncologist he believed could help him beat the cancer. My daughters were 2 and 3 years old, and that chronic sense that nearly all working mothers have of being neither a good parent nor an effective worker was exacerbated by my feelings of failure as a dutiful daughter. No one, not loved ones or colleagues, was receiving the kind of attention I felt they were owed. My dad was disappearing before my eyes. I barely touched base with my kids and my husband, who had his own high-pressure job as editor-in-chief of *Spy* (and was himself working under trying circumstances dealing with new owners based in Europe). I felt dissociated from the easy collegiality of my colleagues, strung out and brittle.

Dad died as I was beginning the negotiations for the Sony deal. And then, eight months later, as the deal was in its closing weeks, a neighbor of my parents called me to say that my mother had collapsed and was in an ICU. I began to lose it. I started self-medicating with alcohol. I was numb and confused about how to process my feelings *and* the conflicting demands on my time—the need to be there for my little kids, to be a wife, to support my widowed and now suddenly dying mother, and to do my increasingly demanding job. Compartmentalizing felt like my only option.

And I focused on the easiest compartment to manage: work. Even if I couldn't cope with the feelings of sadness and loss that were overwhelming me, I thought that I could put one foot after the other and at least go through the motions—no, *succeed*—at the office.

On Valentine's Day, just ten days after her diagnosis with pancreatic cancer, my mother died—and so, too, unbelievably, did her own widowed 94-year-old mother, who'd happened to fall down a flight of stairs two days earlier. In less than nine months, I lost both my parents in their sixties, my roots (my only sister lives in Cleveland), and a huge chunk of my emotional ballast. Nearly two decades later, I can scarcely fathom the amount of emotional labor that was necessary for me to show up at work every day and try to act like a normal, competent, emotionally well-adjusted adult.

I offer the details of the toughness of that time in my personal life to illustrate how we never really know what storms are raging, beneath the surface, in the lives of our colleagues. Working didn't *really* make things "okay" for me, but I did find that the matter-of-fact, nose-to-the-grindstone nature of the job at least provided a practical, external focus during a time of tremendous emotional shock and upheaval. I was hanging by a thread, but I was hanging. And the truth is that the predictable structure of work and its nominal unemotionalism offered a beneficial routine that anchored me, and by forcing me to interact with people who weren't mired in my misery, work offered me escape and healthy solace.

WHY BEING HONEST ABOUT COMPASSION IS GOOD FOR YOU AND FOR BUSINESS

I'm not proposing that we turn the workplace into some kind of nonstop group hug. Your job and your private life are *different*.

But encouraging empathy at work can be useful. Neurobiological research is showing that those who psychologically recover more quickly from life's vicissitudes also tend to have more robust immune functions. Moreover, immunity levels can be improved. A recent study at the University of Wisconsin School of Medicine of patients' immune systems found that those treated by doctors who had longer and more extensive interaction with patients, and who subsequently gave their doctors high "empathy" ratings, were able to rid themselves of colds a full day earlier, on average, than those who gave their doctors low empathy scores. In a 2009 study at a long-term health-care facility that looked at the patient, the staff, and the family, Sigal Barsade, the Wharton business school professor mentioned earlier, discovered that "a culture of caring and compassion had a clear positive influence on the residents, who experienced greater satisfaction, higher quality of life, and more pleasant mood." If ordinary, authentic human kindness can improve health, imagine the possible ramifications for all kinds of workplaces. According to the *Journal of Occupational and Environmental Medicine,* in 2007 U.S. businesses reported a total annual cost in lost work and productivity of $63 billion as a result of workdays lost to illness. The potential for cheerfulness on the job to be infectious and money-saving seems plausible. Empathy is good for individuals and good for organizations.

And remember oxytocin? It turns out that it's the hormone, as Natalie Angier wrote in *The New York Times,* that "underlies the twin emotional pillars of civilized life, our capacity to feel empathy and trust." Researchers have discovered that oxytocin is not simply a stimulus to child care but a key enabler of the human ability to read faces and infer the emotions of others. Research is also demonstrating that basing performance *purely* on beating the competition or making money can actually *decrease* employees' intrinsic motivations to pursue a goal. In her book *Rapt: Attention and the Focused Life,* Winifred Gallagher cites a study in which "college students who were paid to do a puzzle were significantly less motivated than those who worked for free."

CAN EMPATHY BE BOLSTERED?

More than twenty years ago, the Dalai Lama and a group of western scientists began a series of dialogues that grew into the Mind & Life Institute, a nonprofit designed "to promote the creation of a contemplative, compassionate, and rigorous experimental and experiential science of the mind which could guide and inform medicine, neuroscience, psychology, education, and human development." One particular area of study for the group has been the science of compassion, and whether the practice of a particular form of meditation could stimulate positive physical and psychological benefits. And the answer seems to be yes. Through a series of controlled experiments studying the active minds of novice and experienced monks while sitting in what is known as "compassion meditation"—where rather than focusing on the breath, which is typical of traditional meditation, the monks think about another person, all sentient beings, or an animal—researchers discovered a significant increase in the production of high-frequency gamma brain waves, the fastest of the frequencies and signifiers of the most intense state of focus possible. Gamma brain waves are found in virtually every part of the brain, and are associated with peak concentration and the brain's optimal state for cognitive functioning. Additionally, the scans derived from the fMRI images of trained monks revealed heightened activity in the left prefrontal cortex, the area of the brain associated with positive emotions such as happiness. And a study by researchers at Emory University published in the medical journal *Psychoneuroendocrinology* suggests that individuals who practice compassion meditation react better to stress and are less inclined to suffer depression.

BUILDING YOUR COMPASSION EMOTION MANAGEMENT TOOLKIT

Given how strenuously we attempt to pretend that the workplace is an emotionally neutral place, it's no wonder that very few people know how to cope when upsetting things happen at work.

EMT—BEING FIRED AND FIRING

Business schools and human resource departments provide next to no useful instruction—other than to instill in every boss the fear of litigation, and thus encourage them to behave robotically. There's no question that being fired and firing sucks, but if the employee feels valued and feels that the person who is firing them can see their *humanity* while treating them with a measure of dignity, then there is a greater chance that both the employee and the employer will suffer less.

- Never put your words into the fired or laid-off person's mouth.
- Allow time for the bad information to be processed.
- Learn to sit quietly with another's unhappy feelings.
- Offer the distressed person a tissue, which is a culturally appropriate gesture of comfort and the workplace equivalent of a child's teddy bear. In short, be compassionate.
- Talk to someone you trust.

EMT—WHEN THE GOING GETS TOO TOUGH

When my parents were so ill, I wish I'd known to ask specific things of my colleagues by saying something like, "I'm having a rough go of it today, so please know that (a) if I'm not paying attention it's not you, (b) I may need to leave a meeting, or (c) I need to leave work early." Remember that almost three-quarters of the people we surveyed said that they *want* to help others at work. Don't be afraid to ask for help when you need it.

And what to do remains the same whether you are the peer, manager, or employee of someone dealing with a challenging personal situation—let them know that you're aware of what's going on. Communicate that what's happening—a dying parent, the diagnosis of an illness requiring treatment, a sick spouse or child—is something universal and human that all of us experience. If you're the supervisor or peer, ask to set up a time to talk about what's going on to try to identify the variables that might affect the person's work and ways in which you can support them. If the situation will require them to change their work schedule, partner with them to identify ways to help make that happen, and try to define the parameters of what is acceptable—how much advance notice is needed, who will fill in, and so on. If the situation affects a range of others at work, help establish ways in which those disruptions can be minimized. Then work with the person to craft language that best expresses what they'd like others in the organization to know about what's going on. Be respectful and *listen.* The more any possible shame or embarrassment can be proactively avoided, the better.

EMT—TRY COMPASSION MEDITATION

As I mentioned in the last chapter, I've tried to meditate, but my anxious, type-A nature makes it very hard for me to sit still. I try to be "good" and empty my brain of specific thoughts, but it's a challenge every single time. But recently I've tried compassion meditation, and using this form, it is far easier for me to lose my sense of mental hurly-burly and maintain my focus. I sit quietly and focus on my "heart center," breathing in and out, imagining a soft green light suffusing my body. I let go of harsh judgments about myself—I don't excuse my behavior, I simply accept it. Then I extend my thoughts toward anyone I wish to have compassion for—it can be my fragile 88-year-old neighbor in Brooklyn, the people of Sudan, or even, say, someone like Sumner Redstone. And I find that I can sit with that emotion and still my mind. And as my mind stills and I project positive feelings onto my subjects, I find my sense of well-being expanding.

SEVEN

Big Girls Do Cry

Tears ease the soul. —Socrates

When a writer I'll call Rebecca Martinez first went to work as a low-level staffer and editor at *Texas Monthly,* everyone was required to attend monthly story idea meetings that she says "were like a Star Chamber." Every month, she had to sit at a long table, with a group that was 90 percent male, all of whom would go on to become major writers and editors. The atmosphere was extremely competitive, and even though the editor was a nice guy, according to Rebecca, the meeting made him nervous, "and when he got nervous he got mean."

As a young, green female writer, Rebecca felt particularly exposed, and worried that if she got too much criticism from her boss she'd risk becoming a pariah, but if she never made story suggestions he might assume that she was unprepared, resulting in an even greater degree of disdain. "When I did finally start talking," she said, "there was so much anxiety in my voice—it was like bleeding in a tank full of sharks." And the tacit rule—which she felt she failed to figure out until much too late in the game—was to never suggest a story idea you really cared about in the meetings because it was destined to be shot down. "The boys would come in for the kill, and my boss, hearing my tentativeness, would dismiss my idea out of hand. That, in turn, would always make me cry."

While the particulars of the scene Rebecca just sketched are unique, what she experienced—feeling outnumbered, dismissed, and humiliated—is familiar to most women. In our Emotion in the Workplace Survey we found that 41 percent of women had cried at work during the past year, and that crying is common among young women (45 percent), pretty rare among men (9 percent), and even rarer among older men (5 percent).

Many women, like Rebecca, become overwhelmed once the tears start. "The problem is that when I cry," she said, "my nose gets really, really red, as do my eyes, and I can't stop. So there I would be in a room full of men, trying not to cry but turning red as a beet and gushing like a waterfall while all the men in the room—twelve or so—tried to pretend that I wasn't crying while going about their business. They all acted the way boys do when Mom's upset." Emotion? *What* emotion? Rather than figure out what so disturbed their colleague, the editor and other men in the room *acted like nothing had happened.*

Penn State psychologist Stephanie Shields describes what Rebecca observed, in *Speaking from the Heart.* "A woman bursting into tears often grabs the male brain's attention and . . . the tears nearly always come as a complete surprise—and extreme discomfort to a man . . . tears in a woman may evoke brain pain in men." According to Shields, "the male brain registers helplessness in the face of pain, and [this] can be extremely difficult for them to tolerate." The crier feels helpless, and because the observer feels that he can't do anything, he, too, feels helpless, which in turn exacerbates the crier's feelings of impotence. "A woman crying at work is more threatening for a man than having someone pull a knife on him," says longtime executive coach Scott Cronin, only somewhat hyperbolically. He says that crying instantly ends a conversation. When a woman cries, men feel confused. Their natural instinct is either avoidance or impulsively suggesting a solution to whatever provoked the situation. Men (and actually many women too) want to do or say *anything* to fill the space while someone else cries.

In other words, it's a spiral of lose-lose. But why? How did such a fundamental biological response become so stigmatized in the workplace?

WHY DO WE CRY?

Tears, because they erupt from within us unbidden, are understood to communicate authentic, unmasked, and unguarded feelings. As infants, tears are one of our few preverbal means of expressing our needs to others—babies cry when they are hungry, startled, tired, frightened, or feeling pain. And while one baby's crying may sound the same as another's to strangers, the quality and intensity of each baby's crying is calibrated to communicate to his or her parents the differences between tears of hunger and tears of fatigue, frustration, or pain. And since parents usually understand what their baby needs and respond accordingly, the tears and their consequences reinforce in parents the feelings of empathy for which we are evolutionarily built to help the survival of our genes. For babies, their tears ensure that their basic needs are met—food delivered, diapers changed, scary feelings soothed. In other words, crying is our earliest communication tool and it is integral to the perpetuation of our species. But it is only within the last decade that the scientific community has really focused on understanding how this whole cycle works.

THE PHYSIOLOGY OF TEARS

Our bodies produce three different kinds of tears: basal, reflex, and psychic. The *basal* kind are actually mislabeled tears, since they are limited to the liquid that continuously bathes our eyes, keeping them moist. *Reflex* tears are irritant tears, those we produce when an eyelash gets in our eye or when we chop onions. The *psychic* tears are the ones that we are interested in here. These tears are an adaptive response specific to emotional states, and contain higher concentrations of protein, making them biologically different from the other two types.

Emotional resilience necessarily requires a good recovery function or reset button—an ability to return to a baseline calm after an emotional outburst—and tears seem to be one of our bodies' chief means of restoring our default psychic chemistries. Crying stimulates the production of dopamine, a neurotransmitter that helps us feel better—and that also reduces prolactin production, which eventually helps curb the flow of tears, resetting our emotional equilibrium. The *physical* process of crying can make the crier feel better. At the same time, observers' brains are washed in oxytocin, the neuroactive hormone that helps create feelings of empathy in response. Everyone should feel better.

From the time of Hippocrates, 2,400 years ago, tears have been associated with catharsis and the body's ability to cleanse itself of bad stuff—humors, moods, and toxins. "Tears," one Hippocratic text declared, "are humors from the brain, and thus any excess needs to be expressed, purged by weeping." The healing power attributed to tears, both physical and emotional, is ingrained in our culture. Therapists encourage patients to "let it out," or "get in touch." There is a widespread belief that bottled-up, unexpressed emotions have the power to hobble or sicken us, capable not only of suffocating our personal growth but also, more dangerously, damaging us by developing into life-threatening illnesses such as high blood pressure, high cholesterol, and ulcers. There is an implicit assumption in our culture that repressed emotions even have the power to harm us.

THE PSYCHOLOGY OF TEARS

Psychic tears aren't specific to any single emotion but are rather the uniquely visible testament that one has experienced something overwhelming—anger, awe, love, fear, pride, embarrassment, or sadness. From the tears of joy at a wedding or the birth of a child to the tears of anger or outrage—often catalyzed by feelings of powerlessness—at a slight, to the tears of grief at the death of a loved one, each emotion elicits a different intensity and duration of crying. Psychic or emotional tears, because they are exceptional, force us and those around us to acknowledge that something important has just happened—my boyfriend proposed to me, my boss yelled at me, I was deeply moved by a sense of the divine, my dog died—and that we should pause and take a moment for reflection. Psychic tears, as in Rebecca's case as a young writer at *Texas Monthly,* can also be helpful adaptively by communicating submission. Tom Lutz, a University of Iowa professor and author of *Crying: A Natural and Cultural History of Tears,* describes such crying as "the human equivalent of a dog putting its tail between its legs—*Please,* we can say with tears, *I am already abased, do me no further harm.*"

In spite of all the benefits of tears, our culture has negative, unaccommodating attitudes toward public crying. Once a child leaves home for a few hours a day at school, crying, which was an accepted and essential form of communication virtually the day before yesterday, is now viewed as disruptive and is only condoned if provoked by a physical injury or ailment. If kids cry at school or in the mall, they are admonished to stop acting like a baby. To be labeled a "crybaby" is anathema. Neither other kids nor adults want to be around "leaky" children. As we age, any extremes on the behavioral spectrum become stigmatized—the too-rowdy child is labeled disruptive, the too emotionally expressive child is labeled needy and high-maintenance. Stiff-upper-lipping becomes the rewarded behavior. And indeed, reining in our emotions as we encounter ever-larger groups of people, dealing with mere acquaintances and strangers rather than family and intimates, is, in fact, a good and necessary thing. Social rules and decorum, up to a point, are what make day-to-day coexistence possible. At work, crying is generally regarded as a nonverbal form of TMI. And unsurprisingly, almost every woman I spoke with during the course of research for this book admitted to having cried at work and wishing that she hadn't.

THE GENDER FACTOR—UNDERSTANDING THE SCIENCE

In general, and not just at work, women cry almost four times as often as men—according to neurologist William Frey, an average of 5.3 times per month, compared with 1.4 times for men. A University of California study in 2001 found that 65 percent of men "almost never" cry, whereas 63 percent of women admit to crying "occasionally" and 18 percent "frequently."

And as a result of our biology at least as much as our cultural shaping, women cry more visibly as well as more often than men. Women's tear ducts are anatomically different from male tear ducts, resulting in a larger volume of tears. "When men cry," writes Frey, "73 percent of the time, tears do not fall down their cheeks," whereas with women almost *every* crying episode involves runaway tears.

Hormones also likely play a part in women being more tear-prone. Not only do tear glands themselves contain prolactin, a female hormone, but there is also evidence that women tend to cry more just before the onset of menstruation and at ovulation.

For many women, frustration, stress, personal problems, and hormonal changes caused by pregnancy, menstruation, or menopause result in unwanted tears that may be unavoidable. It is these unwanted and unavoidable tears that really provoke our embarrassment. We get angry at our inability to control the most basic and vivid expression of our feelings. Erika Andersen, a management consultant and author of *Growing Great Employees* and *Being Strategic,* says that "a person can decide not to scream at someone, but in my experience it is very hard to *decide* not to *cry.*"

THE CRYING TRIBE

My insight into how complicated tears at work can be came first from anecdotal observation. In interview after interview, people consistently started their answers to questions about how they behaved at work by either saying, "I'm a crier, so . . ." or "I'm not a crier, so . . ." I realized that a de facto sub-rosa "tribe" of criers might exist, including a small subset of men, who regularly behaved in ways that were perceived to be outside the workplace norms. Probing the data from the JWT survey confirmed this suspicion. Two obvious categories of people emerged, the criers and the non-criers, respectively constituting 25 percent and 75 percent of the total population—but 41 percent and 59 percent of women. Here are some of their attributes.

The "criers," whether women or men, strongly believe that emotions in general are positive in informing their behavior at work. They more often have female bosses, but also, compared to people who don't cry, consider their bosses to be "assertive." When receiving a negative performance appraisal, criers say that they often feel like "hitting something" (39 percent) and then feel like crying—which corroborates the findings from studies that suggest that crying is often the more socially acceptable secondary emotional response after anger. In the survey, we found that there was a kind of emotional cascade that overwhelmed criers regardless of the provocation. At first they almost always have the urge to express their feelings physically, but when prevented by social custom from doing so, they next feel the impulse to lash out verbally—and then, when constrained by workplace norms from showing anger directly, they end up crying. For criers, in other words, the emotional constraints of work cause crying. Criers also seemed to take slights—rude customers, being unfairly blamed or not properly recognized for their work by bosses or colleagues, other people at work slacking off—more personally.

But it was in the *differences* among the things that made women and men cry that the data also illustrated some important gender distinctions. A large majority of the men (61 percent) who reported crying at work cited *personal* reasons—an illness in the family, the death of a pet—as the catalyst, while a similarly large majority of the women (58 percent) said it was something that happened *at work*—being unfairly blamed or criticized, someone else taking credit for work—that made them cry.

What might underlie these differences?

THE SOCIOLOGY OF TEARS

How we view crying is reinforced early in life by cultural understandings of gender and emotion. In a 1990 study, psychologists Richard Fabes and Carol Martin showed preschool children images of people expressing different emotions. The kids were three times more likely to incorrectly recall the gender of the person in the image if the emotion being shown was perceived as being unstereotypical. According to the results from the study, boys were so uncomfortable with seeing other boys cry that they denied the empirical facts by substituting girls in their memory.

Kimberly Elsbach, a professor of management at the University of California Davis, Graduate School of Management, has spent the last few years studying women and crying in the workplace. Her research shows that frustration and stress can cause crying, but that criticism is the single biggest driver of tears at work. "And that can be a tough one for women, because if you cry in response to criticism it can be seen as a sign of lacking toughness and hardiness and an inability to take the punches."

Our survey results offered some insight into the ways in which men and women differ when responding to criticism. When it was a work issue that triggered tears, for 46 percent of the women it was more the *content* of bosses' or colleagues' critical messages that mattered to them, whereas only 19 percent were most bothered by the *style* of the criticism. Among the men who cried, on the other hand, only 29 percent were mainly upset by *what* was said, while 36 percent said the most upsetting things were the volume and intensity of the message.

Criticism is tough for both genders to process, and while men may suffer self-esteem and health issues from bottling up their feelings, women have the opposite problem—we tend to experience negative effects of our perceived inability to *control* our emotions. Crying when we actually want to get angry, the standard female emotional transmutation, makes us feel doubly bad. In our survey we found that in spite of the physiological benefits of tears, women who cry at work are acculturated to feel significantly worse as a result. And according to Elsbach, "It's an enormous burden women have that men don't have." In sharp contrast, the men in our survey said that after crying, their minds felt sharper, the future seemed brighter, and they felt more physically relaxed and "in control" than before the incident. In short, *women feel worse after crying at work, and men feel better.*

OUR OWN WORST ENEMIES

Because women tend to be ashamed of public tears, and feel obliged to disprove the essentially correct gender stereotype, they often become the most hard-line opponents of public crying. In *Leading from the Front: No-Excuse Leadership Tactics for Women,* former marine captains Angie Morgan and Courtney Lynch are harshly judgmental about women who cry at work. "Tears chip away at your command presence, or your ability to inspire confidence in others through your demeanor. They create a perception of weakness," because "when women lose control of their emotions, this often suggests to their team that they have lost control of the situation." A 2007 study by the British Psychological Society of women crying at work verified this deep-seated modern notion, finding that "women feel embarrassed and ashamed when they succumb to tears at work, for fear of appearing weak or incompetent to colleagues or customers. They feel it reinforces a negative female stereotype."

Our survey data corroborate these findings. We found that 43 percent of women consider people who cry at work "unstable," which sounds like a chronic and serious character flaw, whereas approximately the same number of men (47 percent) see crying at work as merely "unprofessional" behavior, more suggestive of a forgivable one-time lapse.

IN THE REAL WORLD

"My question is very personal," a sympathetic female voter in New Hampshire asked the candidate in January 2008. "How do you do it? How do you keep upbeat?"

And famously cold, hard Hillary Clinton, figuring that her quest to be president was twenty-four hours from ending, choked up and got teary. "It's not easy," she answered. "You know, this is very personal for me."

As Jodi Kantor wrote about the incident in *The New York Times,* "[By] making a nakedly emotional plea for her candidacy, Mrs. Clinton prompted one of the most fiercely debated moments of the Presidential campaign to date. . . . Americans from across the political spectrum played and replayed the clip, pausing on every flicker of expression on Mrs. Clinton's face, and asking questions like: After a political lifetime of keeping her emotions secret, why was Mrs. Clinton finally letting her guard down? Was it a spontaneous outburst or a calculated show? Was Mrs. Clinton using her gender to win sympathy or was she the victim of a double standard that allowed male candidates to cry—several have on the trail—but not female ones?"

According to Clinton, it was a spontaneous outburst. "I actually have emotions," she said on CNN between the tears and her surprise New Hampshire primary victory. "I know that there are some people who doubt that." And on another program she said that the megacoverage of her emotional moment showed "the double standards that a woman running for president faces. . . . If you get too emotional, that undercuts you. A man can cry; we know that. Lots of our leaders have cried." *Such as, oh, say, her husband, when he was president.* "But a woman, it's a different kind of dynamic."

My interviews for this book have confirmed again and again that Hillary Clinton's experience is not unique. A woman crying at work—and Clinton was most definitely at work when her tears came—remains both routine and taboo. A prominent entertainment executive confessed to me that during job interviews she asks her prospective assistants, who are almost exclusively female, if they're the type to cry at work, since she doesn't want to hire the kind of person who regularly goes to the bathroom to cry and leaves her phone unattended. A female executive at Goldman Sachs described a female partner who referred to the last stall in the ladies' bathroom as her "office"—where she retreated to cry *every afternoon* after the market closed. On her first day as an intern at Johns Hopkins Hospital, Mindy Shapiro, who is now a pulmonary specialist practicing at a Kaiser Permanente hospital in northern California, was shown around her station by her female superior, a resident, who specifically pointed out the three closest women's bathrooms—what she called the crying rooms. "*Never* let the men see you cry," the senior doctor told her. "If you do, they will view it as a sign of weakness and mistrust you." And let's not forget that during her spin-off of *The Apprentice* in 2005, Martha Stewart told a woman, "Cry and you are out of here . . . women in business don't cry, my dear." The title of fashion public relations maven Kelly Cutrone's bestselling book, *If You Have to Cry, Go Outside: And Other Things Your Mother Never Told You,* says it all—tears at work are still verboten.

In my very first adult job, as an administrative assistant at the New York City headquarters of a commercial bank, my desk, on the hushed, deep pile–carpeted executive floor, was a few feet opposite the bathroom doors—lowest in the pecking order but an ideal place to observe the office's channels of emotional overflow. I spent hundreds of hours watching those doors, noting again and again as the three senior women on the floor rushed into the bathroom and reemerged after a beat too long with the remnants of a good cry still visible on their splotchy faces. And it was clear from their almost aggressive glares if I happened to catch their eye that I'd better pretend like nothing out of the ordinary had happened. These first female role models of my professional life were plainly ashamed of their tears.

By and large the women who caution most strenuously against tears at work, those who are intolerant of them to an exceptional degree, are older and part of the battle-scarred early generations of women who had to emulate the narrow-band male emotional spectrum to gain entry to the professional arena. What worked for them became the reflexive, uncritical norm for those who followed. That norm fails to take into account the biochemical differences between the genders and between the tribes of people who view themselves as either non-criers or criers.

When a non-crier works with a crier, interactions can be challenging. Now the editor in chief of *Reader's Digest,* Peggy Northrop's experience with a hard-to-manage, wear-her-emotions-on-her-sleeve assistant when she was editor of *More* magazine exemplifies how this difference in style can play out. While Peggy was very fond of the young woman, "she and I could not have been more different. She was very talented but also comparatively out there with her emotions. She would cry, she'd get mad—and as a result she is one person to whom I've given a talk about emotion regulation. I suggested to her that she slow down—because I thought such emotional vacillation could be a detriment to her career."

Similarly, author Sara Nelson, former editor in chief of *Publishers Weekly,* makes it very clear that it isn't only men who are undone by female colleagues who cry. She described a female employee at the magazine who was "a big crier." "The first few times she cried in my office," Sara said, "I freaked out, but after a couple of times of this behavior, I found myself getting mad in advance because I felt like she was trying to manipulate me. I ultimately got to the point where I said, 'Fuck it. No matter what I say she's going to cry,' so I became inured to it." In this instance, the crier's tears were viewed so negatively that they triggered precisely the opposite result from their presumed intention, *less* empathy instead of more. The boss's resulting disengagement means that whether or not the employee's issues are valid, at a certain point *they will no longer be heard.*

What none of these examples take into account is the fact that to be human is to cry. It can be an essential physical and emotional release, and it's perhaps the most effective tool we have to communicate that we are seriously distressed. It's who we are. Author and management consultant Erika Andersen puts it well: "No one wants to cry at work. But if you say to yourself, 'I know people will sometimes get overwhelmed, and if that happens one or two times a year, can I handle that?'—well, the answer is 'Yes, of course I can handle that.' " Indeed, she added, "crying at work is transformative and can open the door for change."

BUILDING YOUR CRYING EMOTION MANAGEMENT TOOLKIT

That tears can be transformative is one of the main points of *It's Always Personal.* Each of us needs to understand that tears communicate the fact that something in our lives is out of kilter right now: we are overworked, we are sick, we feel taken advantage of, we are angry, we are frustrated. *But we are not weak people or failures.* What matters is that we step back, rationally, without undue judgment, and figure out what is going on. Don't ignore the tears. Use the occasion of crying to analyze and assess.

EMT—HANDLING TEARS

You've just burst into tears; now what? If you are in a group—on the floor of a department store, serving a table in a restaurant—quietly excuse yourself and then, rather than shutting yourself away in your office or the bathroom and stewing over the situation, I suggest taking a walk outside. This approach, just as it does after an outburst, will give you a different perspective and some fresh air and sunlight will help clear your mind. The other people going about their daily lives might ground you, putting your problem into a larger context. After taking that physical and psychological break, if possible you should quietly rejoin the meeting, go back to your post, and set aside time after the meeting or the day to approach whoever triggered your tears. Ask for the opportunity to talk with them the next day. The time will allow each of you the chance to step back and think about what happened and why. Pretending that nothing happened will push the issue under the carpet, and the underlying issues will never be sorted out.

If you find yourself crying while you are alone with a boss or colleague, ask them for a moment to compose yourself. Sit quietly, as awkward as that may sound, and then pick up where you left off, unless the situation remains too volatile. In that case, excuse yourself and follow thc suggestions above.

If you are present when someone else cries, the advice is actually the same. In a group, calmly and kindly suggest to the person crying that she or he might want to take a breather and return in a bit. If you're in a one-on-one situation, try not to move on too quickly. Learn to sit with the uncomfortable reality of the situation, offer a tissue, and let the neurochemicals flow and the emotional heat dissipate. Peak emotions don't last long.

In my experience and those of the people I talked with, almost no one reacts this way. What usually happens is that the person who is crying abruptly and wordlessly leaves the room, and everyone has been made so uncomfortable by the experience that the crier never returns. Everyone wants to pretend that it didn't happen, and just wants the awkwardness to go away. No one derives any benefits from a wholly natural, wholly human, and possibly significant experience.

It's far better to destigmatize the tears—accept them for the biological fact that they are, similar to a hiccup, sneeze, or burp, but meaningful. Regard the moment as a yellow flag, a clear signal that there's some problem to be addressed and, if possible, solved.

EIGHT

Beyond the Facts of Life

Why are empirical questions about how the mind works so weighted down with political and moral and emotional baggage? —Steven Pinker

Before turning to the ways in which we can strengthen our emotional resiliency, I want to discuss the broader social and cultural contexts in which our norms for emotional expression at work were created—and how neuroscientific research may shape future thinking about the virtues of emotion in the workplace.

HOW WE GOT TO WHERE WE ARE TODAY

The enactment of the federal Equal Pay Act of 1963 and the Civil Rights and Economic Opportunity Acts in 1964, which guaranteed that no one could be discriminated against in hiring, pay, promotion, or dismissal on the basis of race *or* gender, unleashed a dynamic of vast social change. And that social change, its progressivism notwithstanding, was confusing and disconcerting to almost everyone involved.

The law mandated that we all be treated equitably at work. But intention, of course, doesn't immediately redefine practice. Since men overwhelmingly controlled the protocols and structures of life outside the home, how men conducted themselves at work became the de facto standard for women to follow. While ostensibly no woman could be denied employment for which she was qualified, there were no clearly articulated guidelines for precisely how men in the male-dominated world of work should actually manage the integration of this new cohort of people who have inherently different operating styles. Because men were the dominant majority, "equal under the law" for women at work pretty much meant the freedom to behave as much as possible like men.

No doubt it was discombobulating for men when women first entered the workforce as nominal equals. Would women take their jobs? How would men handle the introduction of more complicated levels of sexuality into the workplace? Would demystifying the workplace for women deprive men of some kind of priestly fraternal power? Would women mess up the one neutral place where adult men could bond mano a mano? It's unsurprising that men and society at large concluded that the only practical way for men to treat women at work was to embrace and enforce a blinders-on policy in which it was easiest to treat women as if they were, at best, men wearing skirts.

And if there was no general understanding or consistent rules in the sixties and seventies—and even into the eighties—for how the entrenched, mostly male workplace culture should accommodate the surge of new female colleagues, beyond rudimentary obligations to provide equal pay and opportunity, the subtler codes of conduct for how women should comport themselves were even murkier. Indeed, I think women's confusion and unreadiness was probably greater than men's as they entered the workplace in great numbers. Should women wear skirts or pants? Jackets? Necktie-ish accessories? Was it okay for a woman to tear up at work or celebrate a colleague's birthday with a home-baked cake? Was makeup a good or bad thing? Could a woman touch a man in any way without crossing some line of appropriateness—and vice versa? Could a woman show anger without being labeled a bitch—and if so, how much? Would acting the concerned, friendly way they might outside the workplace undermine women's credibility on the job? It was a minefield for women.

Men had the comparative luxury of continuing to act more or less the way they always had, that whole hail-fellow-well-met kind of thing. Women, on the other hand, were obliged to adopt and adapt to male standards for professional behavior—and mainly bland versions of them at that. To be successful, many women had to deny and suppress distinctly female parts of themselves—their nurturing impulses, their essential femininity, aspects of their intrinsic emotional biology.

For a new generation of women who are too young to remember, the female archetypes on *Mad Men* have brought the early 1960s vividly to life, a time when women still made up less than a third of the U.S. workforce. It was a time of struggle, when women were overwhelmingly consigned to lower-level jobs, and our modern women-at-work era was still only a speck on the horizon. Over the course of three seasons, Peggy Olson, the pioneering young copywriter character, resolutely advances from her job as demure secretary to Don Draper, the inscrutable, imperturbable, and philandering male creative head, to become the first female on his creative team. But to become that executive Olson sheds her more "girly" aspects, toughening up as she perhaps subconsciously mimics Draper's cards-perpetually-close-to-the-vest version of the successful executive. As Olson rises higher within the agency, she discovers that she's not wholly welcomed into her new male cadre, while she's also becoming increasingly isolated from any easy camaraderie with her former female peers. Olson is contrasted with women such as Joan Holloway, the office administrator character, who is also smart and competent but who, by using the full arsenal of her sexuality to her advantage, is thus considered too conventionally feminine by management to get very far out of the secretarial pool. Holloway's abrupt demotion back to the secretarial-only ranks after brilliantly stepping up to assist with the firm's newly formed television division and successfully managing both jobs was one of the most compelling depictions I've seen of how impossible it was during that era for an overtly feminine woman to advance.

Claire Shipman and Katty Kay suggest in their 2009 book, *Womenomics,* that although the opportunities for women today are vastly greater than those portrayed in *Mad Men,* some aspects remain the same. "[W]omen do not usually feel comfortable with the power structures in their organizations. Hierarchy itself, and its implicit positioning of people into one-up, one-down positions, is actually far from women's search for establishing a series of relationships between equals, as Georgetown linguist Deborah Tannen has effectively documented. So they refuse to get involved. They disdain politics as 'being about self-promotion and power-grabbing, or they go to the opposite extreme, getting so involved that they fight more bloodily than men and leave casualties, male and female, in their wake.' "

Can science help us understand which of these norms are mostly learned and which are biologically intrinsic?

SCIENCE IS NOT POLITICALLY CORRECT

Equal-rights legislation and judicial decisions of the last several decades have been supremely important in establishing a more level playing field for women to enter and succeed in the workforce. Yet an unintended consequence of mandating that women cannot be discriminated against "on the basis of sex" or "because of sex" has been to discourage any general acknowledgment of the recent discoveries of real neurological differences. And while it may be awkward or politically incorrect to discuss biological differences that women and men bring to the workplace, it seems obvious that gender-specific hormones, like the testosterone that bathes men or the estrogen that bombards women during monthly menstrual cycles, make for very different typical emotional states.

Women give birth. Duh. But as a society we haven't fully come to grips with the implications of this for work. Dr. Louann Brizendine devotes considerable space in *The Female Brain* to what women experience on a physical level during childbirth, and graphically describes what it means to an organization to have a mother back on the job twelve weeks later. I was shocked to discover that, according to Brizendine, new mothers lose the equivalent of *four months* of work in lost hours of sleep, that breast-feeding can seriously interfere with mental focus, and that "a woman's brain size returns to normal only at six months postpartum." Excuse me? Pregnancy and childbirth cause our *brains* to *shrink*? Furthermore, new mothers' bodies are coping with unprecedented levels of hormones, and as they wean their babies and return to work, they begin to lose the compensating soothing flow of the stress-reducing hormone oxytocin just as they reenter that high-stress environment. New mothers have to climb up from a real biological deficit just to return to their baseline mood and competency levels. Going back to work without this kind of self-knowledge is like going into battle without any weapons.

What's more, most women in the United States get pregnant in their late twenties or early thirties—often the point when they've advanced beyond an entry-level stage in their jobs and are poised to take their careers to the next level. Pregnancy and all its concomitant volatile hormonal mood swings can wreak havoc with their steadiness and composure—adding yet another psychological stressor to their already burdensome physiological level.

Yet it isn't just mothers who undergo significant hormonal changes at birth, according to Brizendine. As the birth of his child approaches, a father, on average, undergoes a 20 percent spike in prolactin, a hormone that helps enable general nurturing feelings (and, in women, lactation), increasing sensitivity and alertness. Then, in the first weeks after birth, fathers' testosterone plummets by a third, while their estrogen level climbs higher than usual. These hormonal changes prime their brains for emotional bonding with their helpless little offspring.

And so, simply as a result of the four million babies born in the United States every year, many millions of American workers—all those babies' nearly eight million parents—are emotionally stressed and at a disadvantage professionally. Paternity leaves and longer maternity leaves are not, then, simply PC modern niceties, as some of us think, but sensible accommodations of basic biology.

Taking this a step further, think of the organizational and personal burdens we might ease if we felt comfortable acknowledging and accommodating *other* neurobiological realities on the job. While it might open an uncomfortable and potentially contentious can of worms, what might happen in the workplace if we could honestly address these real, scientifically recognized gender differences?

For instance, might there be a benefit for women—and for the places they work—if we could structure work to take better advantage of our hormonal cycles? Recent studies have revealed that during the week immediately preceding ovulation, when women have the most estrogen in their systems, they also have increased verbal capacity because the frontal and temporal regions, major relay stations for processing language in the brain, are highly estrogen-sensitive. In fact, *Scientific American Mind* cited a study conducted by neuroscientists at the University of California at Berkeley that reported that "hormone fluctuations during a woman's menstrual cycle may affect the brain as much as do substances such as caffeine, methamphetamines or the popular attention drug Ritalin." It seems that estrogen triggers the release of dopamine, and dopamine is tied to improved cognition.

A study led by Doreen Kimura, a psychology professor at the University of Western Ontario, established a relationship between the normal hormonal fluctuations in a woman's menstrual cycle and her ability to perform certain tasks—specifically, high estrogen levels improved verbal performance. In *The Venus Week,* Dr. Rebecca Booth, an ob-gyn, writes that "when estrogen is high during their cycle, women are more at ease with themselves. They are more confident performing tasks and accomplishing goals and more socially agile and able to articulate themselves more fully and clearly (due to estrogen's positive effect on verbal memory)."

Then there is the provocative 2007 study conducted by psychologist Geoffrey Miller of the University of New Mexico, who found that dancers at strip clubs earned on average $70 an hour in tips during their peak monthly days of fertility, versus $35 while menstruating, and $50 during the days in between. Miller postulates that men unconsciously find women more attractive during ovulation. "If you're a woman in any service-industry job looking to maximize your tips," he said in an interview, "it might help to know about this so you can exploit these effects."

But it's not just women who would do well to acknowledge the real-world effects of their hormonal fluctuations. Psychologist J. Philippe Rushton, also of the University of Western Ontario, discovered in a 2006 study that men, too, might benefit from an awareness of their own hormonal cycles, since testosterone stimulates connectivity between neurons. Men have seasonal testosterone cycles, with generally higher levels in fall than spring—and, for instance, those levels vary inversely with spatial ability. Rushton suggests that this could make as much as a fifty-point difference in boys' math SAT scores, for instance.

Taken from a different vantage point, *too much* testosterone in male employees might threaten a company's overall stability. In 2007 a task force of researchers from the departments of physiology, neuroscience, and business at Cambridge University discovered that the higher the levels of testosterone in a group of male financial traders, the greater their risk-taking. The study concluded that high testosterone levels "may shift risk preferences and even affect a trader's ability to engage in rational choice." It's an interesting feedback loop—high levels of testosterone lead to greater risk-taking, and larger financial risk leads to greater pressure on the traders, which produces more of the stress hormone cortisol, and both testosterone and cortisol in excess can *impair judgment.*

I realize this is science fiction-y speculation, faintly eugenic-seeming, about a time when biological manipulation leads to enhanced human performance—or, worst case, where the information can be used to discriminate. But I'd like to think that today, with U.S. women irrevocably at work and now constituting more than half the labor force, we can safely raise these kinds of questions without endangering progress. Wouldn't it be better for all concerned if each of us could harness these insights, and, where we have a measure of autonomy or the ability to self-schedule, learn how to improve our own performance and that of our teams?

In fact, there's an irony here. What I'm proposing is that when it comes to emotion and work, we should start being more unflinchingly analytical and empirical than ever before. As science discovers, confirms, and refines new facts about gender-based aspects of emotion, let's try not to react to them too *emotionally,* with either automatic cries of *"Sexism!"* or neo-Victorian *"Ooh, ick"* squeamishness. The truth could set us free.

NINE

The Four Profiles—Which One Are You?

When an inner situation is not made conscious, it appears outside as fate. —Carl Jung

We all—naturally, but incorrectly—assume that others experience emotions exactly the same way we do. But when we step back for just a moment we realize how singular each of us is. And while my first round of research gave me and my JWT colleagues a generalized overview of emotion at work, the data led us to wonder what drove the personal "decision trees" that people follow when they're deciding how to deal with strong emotions at work. And so a year after we conducted our first survey, we launched a second survey, the results of which we turned into what we're calling the Workplace Emotion Evaluation Profile (WEEP). In this phase of research we probed in more granular detail people's individual work styles, the nature of the workplace stresses they face, and how they cope with those stressors. Participating were 818 women and 421 men from all corners of the working world, from senior managers down to entry-level laborers, and from every U.S. state.

Many of you are familiar with the widely used employment-oriented personality test, the Myers-Briggs Type Indicator, developed in the 1920s, which classifies people according to whether they're more extroverted or introverted, and logical or emotional in the ways they perceive and judge the world. (As it happens, Myers-Briggs was first developed by an American mother-daughter team during World War II to assess and guide women entering the labor force for the first time.) The new WEEP matrix we've developed builds on those kinds of basic Myers-Briggs dimensions but also operates in two additional, very specific fields—how an individual processes strong emotions, and the consequences of the resulting behavior in the workplace. The idea is to give you some useful insights into how you and different people—your bosses, your peers, and your underlings—are differently predisposed to act and to deal with strong emotions at work.

With WEEP you can identify the ways you tend to deal with workplace emotion and get a fix on your level of emotional resiliency—and, I believe, supplement your natural, default styles with strategies that can allow you to be a more effective employee or manager. Here is a subset of the thirty-eight questions we asked. For each of the questions, we asked respondents to answer whether they strongly agreed, somewhat agreed, didn't agree, or strongly disagreed with the following statements.

- I feel anxious a lot.
- When I am feeling strong emotions, I find it hard to think about anything else.
- I worry about living up to the expectations of others at work.

- I believe success is more about luck (who you know, being in the right place at the right time) than hard work.
- I don't know why, but people often take what I say the wrong way.
- At work, I tend to defer to the opinion of my superior, even if my view contradicts theirs.
- I'm happier than most people I know.
- Overall, I'm pretty satisfied with my life.
- I'm kind of a pessimist; I tend to assume the worst.
- At work, it's important to me that I am appreciated.
- It's important to me that people like me.
- I could be more successful at work if some of the people I work with weren't so annoying.
- I frequently feel stressed at work.
- I tend to make decisions based on logic and facts.
- I am introspective—I know myself well.
- When someone at work does something that bothers me, I usually say something to him/her about it.
- I am comfortable speaking up at work when my opinion is different from most.
- I prefer working by myself rather than in a team.
- Once I've made a decision, I rarely have second thoughts.
- If I'm annoyed or angry at work, it would be pretty hard to tell because I don't show it.
- In times of stress I find comfort or peace in religion.
- I rely mostly on my feelings to guide my decision-making.
- I easily express my feelings and emotions.
- I like my life to be pretty much the same day to day.
- I consider myself a creative person.
- When I'm stressing out at work, it's usually because of something going on in my personal life outside of work.
- I tend to be pretty competitive with others at work.

- I tend to talk more than I listen.
- I do my best work under stressful conditions.
- I hate to admit it, but I'm a bit of a procrastinator.
- When I'm bothered by something, there are only a couple of people that I'll talk to about it.
- It's more important to be diplomatic than truthful.
- Sometimes when I'm talking with others I feel like I'm the only person who sees the big picture.
- When forced to compromise my principles I still feel a nagging sense of regret.

If you'd like to take the test and see where you fall in our WEEP typology, you can do so online at www.annekreamer.com. You may want to do so now before reading about our results.

WHAT WE FOUND

Two main groups emerged from the data. In the first group (60 percent) were people who tend to be unable to easily shrug off or move past strong emotional reactions and who further divided into two subgroups that we're calling *Spouters* (21 percent) and *Accepters* (39 percent). And the second group (40 percent), featuring those who have comparatively strong inner fortitude and emotional resilience, is comprised of two subgroups, those we call *Believers* (27 percent) and *Solvers* (13 percent).

The first interesting insight the data revealed to us is that Believers and Solvers tend to be optimists, while Spouters and Accepters tend toward pessimism. It was beyond the scope of the survey to determine whether this was a chicken versus egg kind of phenomenon. It may be that optimistic people (remember Cyndi Stivers from Chapter One) tend to accomplish more, which reinforces in them a level of optimism, whereas by anticipating failure naturally pessimistic people fail to try new things.

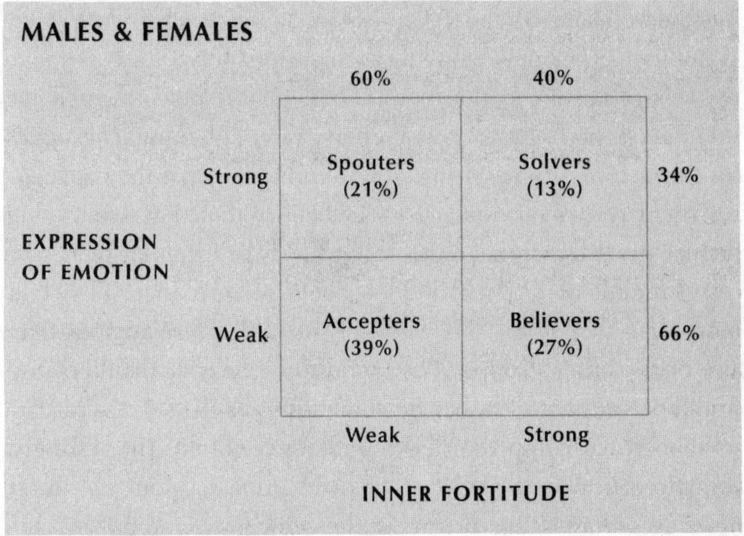

I explain in detail later how to interpret these findings and how to apply them to yourself and people around you. As it turns out, no one category is disproportionately male or female—there is relatively even gender distribution throughout the four categories. But it's crucial to keep in mind as you read about the groups that being mainly a member of one category or another is not necessarily predictive of occupational success or happiness.

SPOUTERS

Spouters (21 percent) are charismatic and exciting, saying more than members of any other group that people "tend to follow what I do more than they follow others." The typical Spouter considers herself a "creative person." They are fun to be around, and their natural energy can enliven tough situations, yet while only one in five people is a Spouter, the ways in which they express their feelings, wearing their emotions on their sleeves, undoubtedly cause them to be responsible for a seemingly disproportionate share of the emotional incidents in the workplace. Whether or not one is enjoying their company, Spouters can take up a lot of the air in the room. These people tend to challenge themselves and—primarily—others, often blaming colleagues for whatever is going wrong. They tend to feel that they have insufficient power even though they believe that they see the big picture more clearly than others. Spouters believe that their success is mainly about luck, and less about performance. They talk more than they listen. They are considerably more anxious than any of the other groups. They tend to be heavier drinkers and smokers, and would rather hit something for the sake of catharsis than reach compromise through conversation. Interestingly, compared to people in the other three groups, Spouters are far more accommodating of tears in the workplace, and not just because they tend to provoke them. Spouters also cry at work themselves significantly more than any of the other three types. Spouters probably benefit the most from body-mind relaxation techniques that can be effective in helping to manage the stresses that often trigger tears.

ACCEPTERS

Most entry-level and mid-level employees fall into the Accepters category, the largest of the groups (39 percent). They are extremely concerned about details, but this attention to detail can be a positive quality, ensuring that careless mistakes are avoided. Rather than lashing out like Spouters, Accepters keep their emotions hidden. Like Spouters, Accepters admit to feeling anxious and depressed. Unlike Spouters, their fellow pessimists, Accepters do not consider themselves creative or natural leaders. They assume that bad things are going to happen, they often don't feel in control of their environment, and they are reluctant to take risks, hedging their bets rather than coming down firmly on one side or another in a disagreement. Given these feelings, it is unsurprising that Accepters tend to procrastinate. They believe it is more important to be diplomatic than it is to be candid. Accepters feel underappreciated and are people who colleagues tend to consider "passive-aggressive." Extenuating circumstances, office politics, and client relations often create intense pressure on people, driving them to behave as Accepters.

Accepters need help to put into words what they are feeling. While we were able to capture their attitudes in the anonymous WEEP survey, in the one-on-one interviews for this book, I found it hard to get Accepters to tell illustrative personal stories about themselves at work—after all, they are people who tend not to reveal their feelings. Many of the people I interviewed who felt the most despondent about their inability to effect change at work described in vivid detail how supportive and effective talking with a good friend or partner had been in helping them manage their emotions. So if I could offer one piece of advice that might help Accepters, I'd suggest that they talk to a trusted friend whenever they feel distressed.

BELIEVERS

Believers (27 percent) think of themselves as relatively happy people who find solace by trusting in the stabilizing, civilizing power of larger principles and the greater good—their faiths, their organizations, their ideals, their country—and feel unhappy when those values are compromised. Being appreciated for their work and staying true to their mission and their principles are central. Believers possess high degrees of fortitude, deriving their most important sense of inner strength from external sources, such as religious belief or commitment to causes. Most Believers don't consider themselves natural leaders, but they are by and large satisfied with their lives. This group skews slightly female. Believers have a solid sense of self. They're less comfortable as a group than Solvers or Spouters with their own expressions of emotion, but they are comfortable with others expressing emotion in the workplace. Unlike Spouters, these people listen more than they speak, and prefer to tell the truth, but don't tend to go out on a limb to make a point. They fall back on the foundations of their social networks to find personal resiliency. Believers can be helpful in emotionally charged situations: during stressful times at work, they can help lift others out of the immediacy of a single moment and help the organization focus on the larger mission.

SOLVERS

Solvers (13 percent) are the rarest in our typology, and relatively more of them are CEOs and business owners than those in the other three groups. Solvers have an inner strength that comes from their sense of personal mastery. Compared with our three other categories, there are twice as many Solvers in top management—owners, CEOs, and other senior executives. They identify themselves as introspective and as people who do their best work under stress and are comfortable speaking up. Solvers consider themselves creative, and are significantly more satisfied with their lives than any other group. They're also, on average, between five and nine years older than members of the other groups—indicating that we may grow into better emotional management as we age. Rather than merely reacting to external events over which they feel little measure of control, these people are problem-solvers—confident in their abilities to get the job done. And they are comfortable expressing emotion as well as observing emotion in others. Solvers are great at thinking under pressure, understanding that work situations and conflicts are inherently complex, never binary. But once Solvers arrive at a decision, they rarely have second thoughts, and can appear aloof and removed from others' concerns or issues.

WHAT KIND OF WORKPLACE EMOTIONAL PROFILE DOES OUR TEST ASSIGN TO ME?

According to the WEEP diagnostic, I am a "Spolver," as it were—part Spouter, part Solver, and only very slightly an Accepter and Believer. My Spouter traits? I worry about living up to the expectations of others. I frequently feel stressed at work. I tend to talk more than I listen. I don't suffer fools easily. And I feel as if I see the big picture more clearly than others. The part of me that's a Solver is mostly satisfied with life, comfortable speaking up at work, and creative. My Solver self rarely has second thoughts, isn't a pessimist, and doesn't procrastinate. In my desire to be appreciated I am also a bit of an Accepter, and I experience real unhappiness when my principles are compromised, which means that I have a toe in the Believer square as well. I have to say that the profile accurately captured who I am, and highlights possible red-flag areas for me in the future—to be wary of taking things too personally, to be aware of my need to be liked and my desire to please others, to think about proactive ways I can lower my stress levels, and to pay attention and *listen* when others speak.

Participating in the survey allowed me to understand firsthand that most of us are, like me, *hybrid* types on the WEEP matrix. I assume that most of us want to imagine that we are clearly one type or another, but it's the rare individual who is any one pure type. Most of us, too, probably hope to be members of the optimistic Solvers or Believers quadrants, but remember as you take the survey that the attributes of the looking-a-situation-squarely-in-the-eye of an Accepter or the let's-get-this-party-started qualities of a Spouter are also valuable assets in a productive work environment. Taking the WEEP survey allowed me to assess aspects of my emotional constitution that might be wanting—a certain lack of resilience in the face of adversity, perhaps, that I might learn to augment and at the same time a level of bluster that might be beneficial to tone down.

IS ANY GROUP "BETTER"?

In addition to examining the emotional traits of each group, we analyzed whether those traits affected success at work, and we discovered that there are successful people within each group, and that among the three non-Solver categories, average income levels were roughly similar.

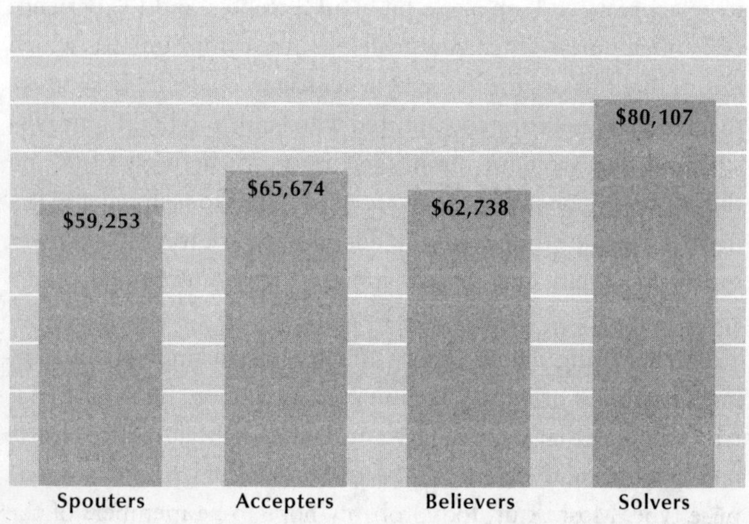

And what percentage of each group were owners, directors, or executives?

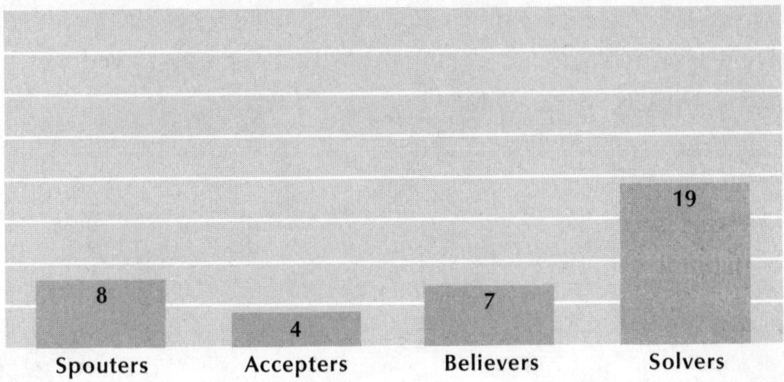

Nor does native optimism necessarily correlate with contentment. Optimistic Solvers and pessimistic Spouters both "agree strongly" with the statement "I'm happier than most people I know."

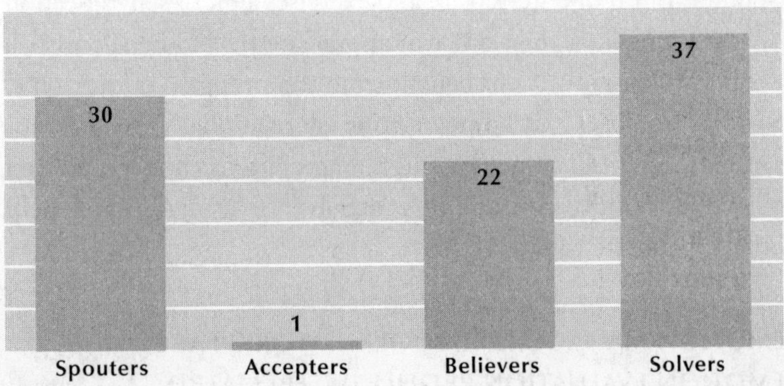

It was also fascinating to note that, perhaps somewhat counterintuitively, Spouters view themselves as strong leaders. The chart following reflects the percentages of people who stated that they "strongly agreed" with the statement "People tend to follow what I do more than they follow others."

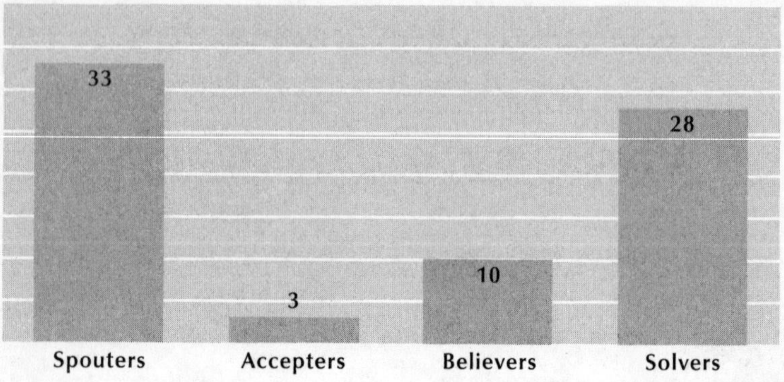

As I've said, people tend not to inhabit one quadrant exclusively, but rather move between the categories as circumstances change. One might feel and behave mostly like a Believer or Solver until pushed beyond one's limits by a particular work situation, at which point one might become, perhaps temporarily, a Spouter. But if one steps back and exercises a bit of self-reflection or metacognition, then one can appreciate that to be successful, people and organizations benefit from the strengths of each type. Spouter qualities can be powerfully motivational. Accepter observations help manage unrealistic expectations. Believer-shared objectives build community. And Solver pragmatism can help others negotiate rough shoals.

EMOTION MANAGEMENT TOOLKIT/WORKPLACE EMOTION EVALUATION PROFILE (WEEP) MATRIX

If you tend to default to one kind of behavior over another and have a feeling that your customary style is not particularly effective, the chart below might prove useful. I've catalogued the various EMTs presented throughout the book (including those from upcoming Chapters Ten and Eleven) according to the dominant emotion that they address and have indicated the profiles for whom those specific strategies might prove beneficial.

EMT/WEEP MATRIX				
	Spouter	Accepter	Believer	Solver
ANGER				
Changing Perspective	✗	✗	✗	
When Is It Okay to Get Angry?	✗		✗	
How to Let Someone Know You're Angry	✗	✗		
How to Apologize	✗			
Metacognition, or Learning to Step Back	✗	✗	✗	✗
FEAR				
Improving Situational Awareness		✗		
Ask for Help	✗			✗
Build Self-confidence				
Value Courage		✗	✗	
ANXIETY				
Just Say "Ohm" or Just Get Moving	✗	✗		
Smell the Roses		✗		✗
What's the Worst That Can Happen?	✗	✗		
Diagram What You Need to Do	✗	✗	✗	✗
COMPASSION				
Being Fired and Firing	✗	✗		
When the Going Gets Too Tough	✗	✗	✗	
Try Compassion Meditation				✗

EMT/WEEP MATRIX				
	Spouter	Accepter	Believer	Solver
CRYING				
Handling Tears	✗	✗	✗	
RESILIENCY				
Write What You Know and Feel	✗	✗		
Assess Your Physical State	✗	✗	✗	✗
CREATIVITY				
Managing Creativity				✗
Nurturing Your Own Creativity		✗		✗

In the real world there is flux, and real people are individuals, with complicated personalities and work situations. It's good to learn what kinds of circumstances or people most challenge you, and then to develop skills for dealing with those situations. Emotionlessness is not the goal, and it's not possible anyway. Spouters are exciting people to work with and for; Accepters' natural skepticism provides checks for our various impulses; the passions of Believers connect us to things with meaning outside our everyday lives; and Solvers anchor us to the here and now, lending stability during times of stress. It's good to be aware of and to know that each emotional style has both positive and negative aspects and that each of us possesses varying degrees of each of the profiles' attributes within us.

TEN

Bouncing Back

Your living is determined not so much by what life brings to you as by the attitude you bring to life; not so much by what happens to you as by the way your mind looks at what happens. —Kahlil Gibran

Thirty-one-year-old Rachel Jacobson, tall and blonde, comes across as the very picture of Midwestern sweetness. Since 2005 she has splendidly executed her vision of bringing excellent movies—new independent and art films as well as classic cinema—to Omaha, Nebraska, through her nonprofit two-screen movie theater, Film Streams. She started her career at Miramax in New York City, working under its cofounder Harvey Weinstein, a notorious Spouter, and after working at that "incredibly aggressive place where yelling and screaming were the norm," Rachel felt that she knew what she *didn't* want in her own organization. Also, as a Midwesterner she knew that "in Omaha, that kind of behavior wouldn't be tolerated."

But unfortunately Rachel found herself succumbing to a classic founder-of-a-start-up mentality, obsessing over every detail and emotionally overinvesting in the outcome of every decision. Since in her mind she'd bent over backward *not* to create an environment like Miramax's, she was kind of surprised when one of her closest colleagues in her five-person office told her that she gets "blamey." As she thought about that comment, she knew that she definitely had her ups and downs, but it was still disturbing to hear that perhaps she wasn't handling the stress of the Film Streams start-up with the grace she had intended.

"I guess part of my problem is that I'm inconsistent," Rachel said. "Sometimes I'm passive-aggressive, and sometimes just aggressive—and I think the staff has a hard time because they don't know from one day to the next, or even sometimes from one minute to the next, how I'm going to be." She recognized that to be a better boss and colleague, it was important for her to develop more personal resiliency and to learn how to be less reactionary to events around her.

Improving emotional resiliency, one's ability to respond to and recover from stressful situations and crises, is critical to gaining greater mastery of our physical and psychological states. Esther Orioli, president of Essi Systems and a leadership development consultant, thinks that resiliency is not so much about *speed* of recovery from emotional assaults but about the *process,* "not just immediately bouncing back like a ball but rather *how* you come back. To me, if you fall down, and deal with the realities and take the time to sort while you are there but you come out over there, well, that's interesting growth. It's plain myth to think that we never have to go to the shadow side." But if you do feel yourself starting to slip to the shadow side and are concerned, there are many ways to come back out.

In a crisis, all of us would prefer to be like Tom Casey, the former American Airlines pilot from Chapter Four who responded methodically and rationally to what he thought might be an on-board in-flight explosion. And just as Casey credits his ability to stay cool to thousands of hours of training, so, too, can one train oneself to develop a greater emotional resiliency. Even the least touchy-feely of organizations has decided that there are benefits to paying attention to our emotions. Responding to an internal 2009 survey showing that 20 percent of combat soldiers show symptoms of PTSD or depression, the United States Army—a culture that Chief of Staff General George Casey says tends to regard "talks about emotions as mollycoddling nonsense"—has just begun incorporating "cognitive development strategies" for increasing soldiers' emotional resiliency into basic training.

Bertrand Russell famously noted that "the degree of one's emotions varies inversely with one's knowledge of the facts." In *Outliers,* Malcolm Gladwell cites the work of neurologist Daniel Levitin, who was the first to identify the "10,000-hour" rule—the idea that "ten thousand hours of practice is required to achieve the level of mastery associated with being a world-class expert—in anything." *Anything?* Including, it seems plausible to assume, emotional mastery. Just remember, change is an evolution, not a single event. If at first you don't succeed—practice, practice, practice.

LEARN TO OBJECTIFY YOUR EMOTIONS

Like Tom, Lynda Resnick, the entrepreneurial powerhouse behind Teleflora Flowers, The Franklin Mint, and more recently POM Wonderful and Fiji Water, in partnership with her husband, Stewart, knows that success is often determined by our ability to prioritize and detail the specifics that inform what might otherwise be seen as emotionally driven enthusiasms. She describes a time of particular stress at The Franklin Mint, when she was running its worldwide marketing, and Stewart, her husband *and* boss as head of sales and operations, yelled at her during a large meeting. Lynda wanted to adapt Raphael's sixteenth-century painting "Transfiguration of Christ" as a piece of Franklin Mint porcelain statuary, but Stewart was unenthusiastic. "I just understood that it was one of the most important icons in the history of art, and I just knew that people would want to buy beautiful religious artifacts, and I had an artist who I knew would do a beautiful job, and still Stewart didn't get it." Instead of throwing a reciprocal tantrum, Lynda was able to remove the emotion from the conversation by commissioning a study that fleshed out the logic behind her otherwise seemingly emotionally based decision, and thus succeeded in persuading Stewart with third-party evidence that there was an enormous untapped market for newly manufactured religious icons. Lynda's intuitive insight into the market, backed up with cogently presented data, ultimately delivered to the company more than $35 million in robust sales for just that one statue.

Lynda's example shows how incredibly effective learning to structure your passionate point of view into quantifiable terms is as a strategy for resolving emotional conflict. Such an approach shifts the conversation from the purely subjective realm and offers people the chance to review the merits of a business opportunity without emotional baggage.

BUILDING YOUR RESILIENCY EMOTION MANAGEMENT TOOLKIT

University of Texas psychologist James Pennebaker has studied the benefits of expressing feelings, and has found that far more than *talking* about feelings, which tends to set us up for unproductive ruminating, *writing* about what's going on helps us comprehensively pin down and organize our feelings and thoughts. And Paul Browde encourages this process, too, as a useful emotional as well as logical therapeutic tool. "There is no need," he says, "even to have a logical train of thought before writing." Even writing something as undirected as "I hate him. How can he do this to me? I am so angry, I could scream, aaaagghhh," can be beneficial, says Browde, because you are externalizing the rage, bringing it outside yourself and onto the page. After a while of expressing emotions on the page, Browde says, "a new clarity will emerge."

EMT—WRITE WHAT YOU KNOW AND FEEL

I asked Mary Prefontaine, the executive director for the Institute for Career Advancement Needs (ICAN), where Rachel Jacobson went for help in developing greater emotional mastery, how one bolsters one's emotional quotient (EQ) and resiliency. Here are a few of the tips she shared with Rachel for developing a stronger, nimbler emotional state. Rather than simply noting your thoughts and feelings and moving on, it's helpful to organize your impressions into a loose outline that can be updated periodically. This will allow you to reflect on any changes in your circumstances over time, setting the stage for tweaks and modifications as you see fit.

- Check in with yourself a few times a day and identify what you are feeling. Mary has found that her clients regularly struggle to find the words that best describe how they are feeling, so this is an important first step. She then encourages them to make a list of both positive and negative emotions and tick off one or two every time they check in with themselves. She says that this labeling really helps people notice what's going on inside.
- As you reflect on what you are feeling, be aware of the immediate things that are causing you stress.

- Identify the people who make you feel confident and who support you, and connect with them on a regular basis.

Here are some questions that I have come up with to help you flesh out your reflections. Experiment and see how much or how little you need to do to make the approach work for you.

- Pay attention to and note your emotional state—anxious, angry, scared, inspired—separating internal stresses, job stresses, and home stresses. Depending on your answers, imagine ways you can address any of the issues you identify.
- Name the key players involved in a project both within your organization and outside. Who is responsible for what? Understand who has the authority to make decisions. Do you know what your job is? What everyone else is to do? Is the authority clear?
- Try to imagine the emotional state of the other key players. Are they feeling secure in their jobs, and about the overall business? Are you aware of any external factors in their lives—illness, pregnancy, financial worries, demanding children—that might require additional sensitivity on your part? Can you anticipate ways to help them deal with their concerns? Should you set up meetings to share those thoughts and solicit their involvement in a resolution?
- What do each of the players stand to gain or lose—both quantitatively and qualitatively—in revenue, in change in status, in headcount, in compensation, and so on? Imagine how each will feel under different outcomes.
- What are the obstacles, and what's not being said? Are resources missing? Are too many people involved, or too few? Is there an insufficient budget? What don't you know? Who can help?

- Is the time frame reasonable?
- How will you be evaluated? By measurable or qualitative means?

Do not use explosive or emotional language in the outline. Keep things as neutral and objective as possible. The outline is *not* meant to be a catchall for vitriol and finger-pointing but rather a tool for presenting in as logical a way as possible the emotional and organizational complexity involved in your work.

Once you have written your outline to the best of your ability, take the time to think about what you've put down. Do you feel calmer, more in control, better able to face whatever obstacles might arise? Has the process allowed you to have a more holistic sense of the project and to identify gaps in your skills, thinking, resources, or knowledge? Can you get help? Do you see any upside that you had not previously identified? Once you are comfortable with your outline, revise it as circumstances and information change. Keep it as a private tool to organize your thoughts and feelings as well as to help you frame potentially difficult conversations with your boss and other colleagues.

As you might have found, making the outline and writing down what you are feeling results in a slight objectifying shift of focus that enables a heightened awareness of one's own emotional state as it relates to whatever project you are working on, and also highlights the possible emotional states of others involved in its execution. That fuller awareness of others is an important element of emotional intelligence.

Imagine the value that Daphne Poser from Chapter Three might have derived from such a document. Remember her sense of impotent outrage when a colleague she felt was less qualified than she was promoted? And how her bosses were incapable of offering her a clear rationale for why the other person was promoted? If Daphne had been documenting the particularly thorny projects she was managing—the elements that were working, those that were not, what the nature of any issues might have been, and how she resolved them—then when she approached her management team she would have been able to present a persuasive argument for her promotion, backed up by documentation detailing when and how she'd overcome obstacles and creatively met challenges. And when the conversation inevitably began to veer toward subjective assessments, she could have used the outline to gently and firmly bring the discussion back to specific business issues.

Or what about Rebecca, the young Texan editor from Chapter Seven? If she'd been recording her feelings over the course of several editorial meetings, specifically capturing how the editor had chosen to shoot down her story suggestions, then she could have scheduled a rationally structured conversation with him describing a pattern of behavior over time. The process of articulating her experience would have established enough distance and perspective for her to remove the "I said, and then you said" potential for rancor from the meeting. It's almost uncanny how something as basic as both parties having an outline on a piece of paper in front of them offers each a device to keep the conversation on track. If Rebecca's boss said something like "What the heck are you talking about?" Rebecca might have calmly said, "Well, if you look here, in fact, on May 2 and July 10, when I suggested x and y, here's what you said. I hope today you might explain in greater detail why you thought my ideas fell short so I won't make the mistake again." And even if you'd never in a million years set up that kind of meeting with your boss, the exercise might nonetheless help you see a pattern in your behavior or inspire insights that can help you avoid similar pitfalls in the future. At the minimum, writing what you feel—objectifying the subjective—will help you develop a perspective on your emotions that can provide the distance that contributes to healthy resiliency.

EMT—ASSESS YOUR PHYSICAL STATE

Whenever I'm feeling unusually brittle or fragile, another thing I do is run a quick body scan—am I hungry, tired, or lethargic? The hormones that course through our glands and brains when we register emotional states produce powerful physical reactions—a pounding heart, a flushed face, streaming tears, and sweaty hands. "Emotions are not only psychological and cognitive," says psychiatrist Paul Browde, "but are powerful *bodily* experiences." For this reason Browde encourages people to notice their physical responses to emotional situations, including rapid breathing, pounding heartbeat, muscle tension, and the desire to lash out. "I counsel people to 'metabolize' the emotion, using deep abdominal breathing, so that it passes more rapidly, and so that the person retains a sense of being in control."

If a few deep breaths haven't helped you feel more in control, make certain that you aren't hungry. It has been found that even slight drops in blood sugar levels can weaken our emotional self-control because our brain requires a tremendous amount of energy to conduct higher level cognitive tasks. If you've ever been in a midday meeting that runs through lunchtime only to find yourself ready to jump down the throat of a long-winded colleague, it could be that your bad mood is merely your prefrontal cortex running low on glucose. And it goes without saying that adequate sleep provides a physical foundation for dealing with the slings and arrows during a day at work. But what is less known is the degree to which the chronic, slightly elevated levels of noise associated with open-plan office spaces can augment stress, wearing down our resiliency. It may be that wearing earplugs, if your situation permits, will improve your focus and your ability to deal with everyday ebbs and flows.

Finally, as ridiculously simple as it seems, smile when it's appropriate. Clinical psychologist Paul Ekman has discovered something extraordinary. "If you intentionally make a facial expression," he says, you tend to "change your physiology [accordingly]. By making the correct expression, you begin to have the changes in your physiology that accompany the emotion. The face is not simply a means of display, but also a means of *activating* emotion."

Ultimately what I'm suggesting is that by monitoring your physical state and creating an emotionally robust outline for major projects or problems at work, you'll be able to discover what psychologist Mihaly Csikszentmihalyi calls "the paradox of discipline and freedom," where one comes to understand that "what feels bad is feeling out of control, and what feels good is feeling under control." Both of these strategies will help foster that sense of control, giving you the resources and at least a provisional map as you make your way through the only partly charted wilderness of daily life at work. Resilience is all about learning to process and then move past the inevitable occasional jolts of negative emotion at work—acute anger, anxiety, fear, and so on—and return to one's emotional normal, ready once again to tackle a job's everyday challenges.

ELEVEN

Happy, Happy, Joy, Joy: Creativity at Work

There is no duty we so much underrate as the duty of being happy. —Robert Louis Stevenson

"It's funny how anger is easier to talk about than joy," said Maud Lavin, a professor at the School of the Art Institute of Chicago (SAIC), when I asked her where she finds the greatest pleasures in her work. "Or at least," she added, sounding very much like the academic precisionist that she is, "it's easier to convey the context of anger than the context of joy." Maud hit on an essential truth about the emotion of happiness. Unlike a fear—for instance, my fear of heights—happiness is hard to isolate, and there's rarely a single, identifiable trigger. At work, apart from the occasional unambiguous triumph—a promotion, a great review, an award—contentment or happiness tends to creep up on people.

Maud's school, SAIC, one of the top graduate arts programs in the country, attracts an outstanding student population of artists of all kinds—painters, sculptors, filmmakers, writers, critics, and performance artists—in their mid-twenties to early thirties. They're often already exhibiting or publishing, so Maud, who's 55, has the pleasure of connecting on a daily basis with young but fully formed adults whom she respects and with whom she shares common passions. As she says, "when there's a good connection in class it feels really fun—it's a connection with younger peers, a feeling of lightness, like you and they are intensely enjoying the same things." As Maud spoke she remembered a great experience from a seminar she teaches called "Lust and Aggression," when a student picked up on a passing comment Maud had made and organized a field trip for the entire class to go to Chicago's Windy City Rollers arena, where female roller derby teams such as Hell's Belles and Manic Attackers compete.

And what was it about the decidedly unacademic outing that made Maud happy? On one level it was simple. She was thrilled that one of her students took the initiative to turn an off-the-cuff notion into a real adventure. But she also loved sharing intellectual discovery and fun with her students. As a group they'd gone from the heavy reading of psychoanalytic texts to closely analyzing films in class to planning this field trip together. Maud and her students found pleasure through what Mihaly Csikszentmihalyi has identified as an important contributing factor to happiness—engaging in new experiences (even outlandish ones like roller derbies) that broaden our horizons. "Whenever we discover new challenges," he writes, "whenever we use new skills, we feel a deep sense of enjoyment. To repeat this desirable feeling, we must find ever higher challenges, build more sophisticated skills; in doing so we help the evolution of complexity move along." Or as Daniel Gilbert put it in *Stumbling on Happiness,* humans have learned to inject variety into their lives to combat habituation, the overfamiliarity that tends to make life boring. "Hey, honey, I have a kinky idea—let's watch the sun set from *the kitchen* this time," is the way Gilbert put it.

As a teacher, Maud also frequently finds contentment through experiencing what Csikszentmihalyi has identified as *flow,* the word he uses to describe what happens when one is completely absorbed in the task at hand. He popularized this notion in *Flow: The Psychology of Optimal Experience,* and described it as that sense of "being completely involved in an activity for its own sake. The ego falls away. Time flies. Every action, movement, and thought follows inevitably from the previous one, like playing jazz. Your whole being is involved, and you're using your skills to the utmost." Of course, a person doesn't just say, "Okay, now I'm going to experience flow" and achieve instant unselfconscious bliss. But in your work you can, with enough mastery (remember the 10,000-hour rule) and by diving in deeply, experience those moments of feeling as if you're in the zone. It's what Maud feels when she teaches a great class, what artists and artisans experience when their work is going well, and what athletes, readers, and lovers feel when they are really immersed in the game, book, or lovemaking—that sense of suddenly looking up to discover that, *whoa,* a *lot* of time has passed. As with Maud, who has logged tens of thousands of hours reading, looking, and writing to build her base of knowledge, as well as practicing and refining her teaching style in the classroom, flow is achieved when the challenge of a particular task is matched by the skill level of the practitioner—and then, sometimes, luck strikes. And luck, it seems, favors the well-prepared.

"I'm good at it," Maud says of her work, "but I also really have to pay attention and pour myself into it. I'm very focused and then tired after teaching that seminar for three hours, but also usually very satisfied. There's an intensity to the discussions, mixed in with humor, that is really, really fun for me, and for them."

That last statement shows that Maud is also aware of another key contributor to contentment—other people. "It's clichéd to say, but it makes my heart happy to share a range of ideas with my students. It's almost a multilingual approach to thinking about culture and being cultural producers. So the happiness is about a kind of *sharing,* intergenerationally." Research supports her anecdotal observation. A 2002 study conducted at the University of Illinois by Edward Diener and Martin Seligman found that the primary characteristics shared by the lucky 10 percent of people with the highest levels of happiness and the fewest signs of depression were their strong ties to friends and family and their *commitment* to spending time with the people they most enjoy. As psychologist Daniel Gilbert puts it, "successful relationships are the key to human happiness."

THE BIOLOGY AND PSYCHOLOGY OF HAPPINESS

Work, like the rest of life, shouldn't be just about coping with the bad stuff. There's also maximizing the good—acknowledging those occasional jolts of occupational joy, savoring the moments of happiness.

Happiness is a state of mind characterized by contentment, satisfaction, pleasure, or joy. There is an intimate connection between seeking pleasure and the reward centers of the brain, and our reward pathways comprise a complicated neural network fed, in part, by the pleasure-activating neurotransmitter dopamine. As with our other emotions, the amygdala, hippocampus, and hypothalamus are also involved. Through studies of brain waves, Richard Davidson, a University of Wisconsin psychologist, discovered that activity in the right frontal cortex or the left frontal cortex tends to be asymmetrical in most people, and the more dominant cortical side tends to correlate with whether a person experiences more positive or negative emotions. As Jonathan Haidt reported in *The Happiness Hypothesis,* "People showing more of a certain kind of brainwave coming through the left side of the forehead reported feeling more happiness in their daily lives and less fear, anxiety, and shame than people exhibiting higher activity of the right side. . . . [T]hese cortical 'lefties' are less subject to depression and recover more quickly from negative experiences." And these tendencies are clear from a very young age. Ten-month-old babies with greater right-brain activity are more agitated and likely to cry when separated from their mothers than babies the same age with greater left-brain activity.

This degree of left or right cortical activity also relates to what is known as your biological "set point." University of Minnesota researcher David Lykken studied 4,000 sets of twins and concluded that about 50 percent of one's basic disposition—easygoing versus stressed-out, for instance—comes from genetic programming. And Lykken found that pretty much no matter what happens to us in life, good or bad, we tend to return to our basic default range.

But fortunately for sensitive types like me, all is not set in stone. Expanding the notion of happiness beyond our genetic and neural predisposition, psychologists Sonja Lyubomirsky, Ken Sheldon, David Schkade, and Martin Seligman have created what they call the "happiness formula":

H (happiness) = S (your biological set point) + C (the conditions of your life) + V (the voluntary activities that you do, from volunteering to sports).

What this means is that while some of our potential happiness is genetically and biologically linked, with some effort we can nudge the other two variables toward conditions that enhance our overall happiness. So what kinds of conditions and voluntary activities favor increased happiness?

While one might assume that affluence and robust health—an optimized value for C in the formula—would dramatically improve one's chances for happiness, researchers have discovered that beyond a relatively modest baseline of money and health, happiness is not very dependent on those variables. As Maud's experience suggests, happiness is equally, if not more, associated with behavior in the V(oluntary) component, which is mostly under one's control—personal relationships, novel experiences, time invested to achieve a level of mastery—and all of which work can provide.

HAPPINESS AND WORK

In her book *The Happiness Myth,* Jennifer Michael Hecht identifies three basic kinds of happiness: good day, good life, and peak, and I've found that thinking about work within her construct has helped me tease apart some of the "happiness formula" variables that influence well-being.

Good-day happiness at work might mean: I got to the office early, I was able to take care of backlogged paperwork that had been nagging me, I had a productive meeting, and I was able to leave in time to make it to my daughter's school concert. Good-day happiness is about an awareness of the fortunate conditions of one's life—where stopping to smell the roses can have measurable positive impact.

Good-life happiness as it relates to work would be more along the lines of being engaged in tasks that you find meaningful and challenging, and in which you are aware that you're helping provide a decent material quality of life for your family. This kind of happiness is more connected to hard work—the sense that one is doing the best one can in any endeavor and, ideally, endeavors in which the work itself is its own reward. Good-life happiness does not relate to things like our gender or our age, over which we have no influence, but rather to conditions over which we do have some control, such as where we work or the kind of work we choose to do. But good-life happiness does not mean that we are "happy all the time," to quote the (only somewhat ironic) title of Laurie Colwin's great novel. Far from it. The positive psychology field puts this in perspective, acknowledging through empirical and replicable research that in spite of the advantages of thinking positively, there are times when "negative" thinking is appropriate, and that difficulty, pain, and sadness are inevitable. To put this in WEEP terms, we need a bit of Accepter apprehension to counterbalance Spouter-like exhilaration. We need obstacles and challenges in our lives for achievements to have meaning, the cold and cloudy days that make us revel in the warm and sunny ones, the necessary and numbing scut work that lets us *really* enjoy the resulting moments of success. Outrage on behalf of the disadvantaged, like that felt by Dickie Davis, the Miami airport executive, can lead people to make their corners of the world better places. Ferocity—a little anger, even—can fuel healthy competition.

And, finally, the third kind of happiness—peak happiness—is the more transcendent sort, by definition rare in everyday life, including (and maybe especially) on the job. I've also found that this sort of happiness becomes more elusive the older we get—the more cares and responsibilities we have, the less willing we may be to engage in the kinds of experiences where peak moments tend to happen. It takes effort to wake up in the middle of the night with our kids to watch the Pleiades' meteor showers if our prospective sense of how exhausted we'll be at work the next day outweighs our anticipation of awe. But, Hecht intimates, it is the peak experiences in our lives that endure, that offer us hope and glimmers of meaning, and that connect us to our families, communities, and a sense of the eternal. And this kind of happiness is closely connected to the "V" in the happiness formula—these are the things we *choose* to do.

While in our personal and private lives peak happiness may be, for instance, the kind of euphoria we experience at a great rock concert or after exceptional sex, at work it is more often connected with the *creation* of something original: designing a new kind of ergonomic desk chair, discovering a new way to isolate and destroy viruses, delivering a giant project early and under budget, or creating the next *Simpsons.* In short, moments of peak happiness at work often involve some aspect of the creative process.

THE CREATIVE CONNECTION

"There have been in my career a handful of times when I had what I call true happiness—where who I was at that time felt in harmony with what my company did and was about," says Tom Harbeck, who is today senior vice president for strategy and marketing at OTX, a consumer research firm. And Tom connects his professional happiness during those times with a few key factors: working for a company where there was "a team of people who 'got it,' " where everyone felt plugged into some larger vision and shared the goal of making the mission come to life. Tom is talking about the same collective experience of flow that Maud did, the happiness derived from face-to-face, day-to-day *social* connection with other seriously engaged people on the same wavelength.

One of Tom's times of peak joy was when he worked at the Chiat-Day advertising agency in the 1980s. "The culture was so intensely alive," he says, "that you couldn't separate the [agency's] slogans from the employees who wore them on their T-shirts. 'Good enough is not enough,' 'I'd rather be the pirates than the navy,' 'How big can we get before we get bad?' It was a culture that thrived on scrutiny, debate, evaluation, and criticism—all aimed at the *work,* not at each other."

Tom was fortunate to find work that tapped into his inner passions. "I was a poetry major," he says, "who had no training in advertising or marketing, in the midst of an organization creating an advertising revolution." Chiat-Day's 1984 Apple ad redefined buzz and event advertising after only one run. Nike's "real athletes" billboards took a 180-degree turn from celebrity sports spokespeople. And the firm's NYNEX Yellow Pages ad, "If it's out there, it's in here," charmed the entire country. Despite Tom's inexperience, his bosses listened to what he had to say and considered *it* (not *him*) against the goal of improving the agency's work, making it closer to great. It turned out that his English-major poetry training—finding and feeling the meaning given an economy of words used freshly—was highly relevant to creating ads. Advertising was intended to make you think and feel something, not unlike poetry. "So despite no prior experience," Tom says, "who I was and what I knew and what I was good at, *at that precise moment in my life,* was valued. I was happy. When it happens, it is tremendous—you cannot believe they actually pay you to show up at your desk; you are giddy."

FINDING CREATIVITY AND HAPPINESS WHERE YOU MIGHT LEAST EXPECT IT

If I asked you to list professions that involve creative endeavor, farming probably wouldn't make your list. But Karen Pendleton, who's 53 years old, disagrees. When first married, she and her husband John farmed 1,000 acres in the Kaw River Valley, in eastern Kansas. Over the years they diversified, leasing some of their land to other farmers to grow the more traditional-to-the-area corn and soybeans, while introducing additional crops like asparagus on the acreage they continued to farm. A devastatingly violent storm in 2006 damaged every building and piece of equipment they owned, destroying their combines and tractors. But rather than give up, the Pendletons took the opportunity to redirect their energies—leasing all but sixty of their acres to neighboring farmers and concentrating on growing flowers and vegetables like asparagus. To their surprise, they discovered that the shift in focus made them happier. As Karen says, "With corn and soybeans you know you're going to plant corn and soybeans and rotate your crops in a set pattern. Everyone plants at the same time, goes to market through the same [grain] elevators, and in general the routine is the same year in and year out." With their invigorated approach to farming, the Pendletons discovered the kind of variety Gilbert identified as being so important to nurturing happiness. "With this kind of farming," Karen says, "there are numerous crops that you can grow and numerous ways that you can market them. You can decide to grow flowers and vegetables or vegetables and fruit seasonally, or year-round through hothouse farming. You can sell your produce through your own stands, via greenmarkets, or directly to restaurants and to local grocers." For Karen, figuring out the optimal kind of marketing for their crops feels deeply creative. "I have all sorts of different ways we can promote ourselves. I use websites and e-mail newsletters and Facebook, and work closely with our community." In fact, it is from their close relationships with their neighbors that Karen finds a source of happiness. "We grow flowers, and I get to design the bouquets for weddings and funerals, and each aspect gives me joy. One day I was handing the bride her bouquet as she was going down the aisle and her dad looked at me and said, 'You have the best job in the world. You get to take people on their happiest day and make them happier.' And to be told that is just an amazing thing." Even where you'd not think to find access to any sort of happiness—a funeral—Karen finds a deep sense of satisfaction. "I did the casket flowers for a gentleman who'd had an implement company," she says, "and his family wanted the flowers to match the colors of his implements, and we [also] included wheat and corn in the arrangement. It was so much more meaningful for the family, knowing that the flowers were local." When Karen and her husband go on vacation they choose places such as San Josc, California, in order to visit cut flower farms, trying to expand their horizons, to learn. Farming is the very hard way she and her family make a living, but it's also, she says, "our hobby." Pendleton's occupation incorporates all the essential rules for finding happiness in work: engagement in a community, a mission, varied experiences, perpetually new challenges, and that enthusiastic amateur-spirit sense that one's vocation can be as much fun as an avocation.

LAUGH AND THE WORLD LAUGHS WITH YOU

As you might imagine, another factor contributing to happiness and creativity at work is humor. Each of us knows this anecdotally and intuitively, of course, but there's beginning to be some scholarly support for the proposition. In London, researchers at University College and the Imperial College have found that laughter is literally contagious. When participants in a study were exposed to a series of sounds ranging from laughter to retching, it was found through fMRI that the positive sounds triggered a strong smile response in their brains' premotor cortical regions, a region responsible for the planning and execution of motor movements, which in turn motivated mirroring behavior among those around them. As Louis Armstrong might have sung, "When you're smiling, the whole world smiles with you."

Okay, fine, a manager might say, jolly employees are all very well and good, but what's in it for my organization and me? How about more effective problem-solving? In an experiment conducted by Alice Isen, a psychologist at Cornell University, one group of test subjects watched short videos of television bloopers, while two other groups performed physical exercise or watched a video about mathematics. Then all the subjects had to solve complicated problems such as being given a candle, a book of matches, and a box of tacks with the challenge of devising a way to stick the lit candle to a corkboard so that it didn't drip wax. Three quarters of those who had seen the funny videos found more creative solutions to the problem than did the math video–watchers or exercisers. Remember Cyndi Stivers from Chapter One, who used a joke to disarm her boss's belittling anger? Her humor allowed her to visualize a different strategy for dealing with anger on the job, the laughter became contagious, and a confrontation was defused.

Danny Meyer, the founder of the Union Square Hospitality Group, opened his first restaurant, New York's Union Square Café, at age 27, and now operates eleven restaurants, a significant special-events business, and even a management-training program. He is among the most successful restauranteurs in the world. In his book *Setting the Table,* he credits his success to exceptional service of a distinctly human, heartfelt kind. "Service without soul," he writes, "no matter how elegant, is quickly forgotten by the guest." And for Meyer, "soul" emerges from a workplace that encourages a maximum degree of personal happiness and self-reflection among its employees. *And* from humor. "Employing a well-timed sense of humor," he told me, "is simply the most effective and universal means of stress reduction and team-building fuel I know. Businesspeople can take themselves so damned seriously—believing that on every decision hinges a momentous outcome—and it's critically important to break the tension with a good laugh every now and then. Happily, a good sense of humor is one of those rare things that society seems to deem equally suitable for both women and men."

Danny gave me a perfect example. "One day I received a brutally candid complaint letter from a disappointed guest at Blue Smoke," he said, referring to his Manhattan barbecue restaurant, "who wrote in great detail about how his wife's birthday had been ruined—despite a warm greeting, a prime table, fantastic barbecue, and timely service—all because their server had neglected to put a candle in the chocolate cake dessert as had been requested (and promised) upon reserving the table." It was the conclusion of the complaint letter that stung Danny the most. He can still quote it. "Blue Smoke has gone downhill, and you can be assured that we will never be back or recommend it to anyone else." Danny wrote a reply with profuse apologies, offering to welcome them back for another meal with his compliments. And then he ripped up the letter. "I knew there was no way that these folks would or could be turned around based solely on a letter of apology, no matter how contrite. And then it hit me: this was a mistake, but it wasn't the end of the world." He chose to write a straightforward apology, acknowledging that the restaurant's error had wrecked what should have been a special moment. And he ended the short letter with one simple word: "NUTS!" He taped the letter to a twelve-jar case of Blue Smoke's peanuts and had them delivered to the man. The next day, he got another e-mail that read like a big hug. "I guarantee he is still telling the story," says Danny, "mistake and all—but the recovery with humor and nuts saved the day."

THE CREATIVITY-HAPPINESS-PROFIT CONNECTION

As Meyer has discovered, it's not merely theoretical, speculative, humane, or "nice" for organizations to figure out ways to optimize the emotional states of their employees and work cultures—it may be an essential way for them to survive and thrive in the new global economy. Especially an economy, as social analyst Daniel Pink describes in his influential book *A Whole New Mind,* in which work has entered the "conceptual age," in which "left-brain" analytic functions can be increasingly performed by computers, and successful enterprises cultivate the " 'right-brain' qualities of inventiveness, empathy, joyfulness, and meaning." If emotion is always personal, and emotion fuels creativity, and creativity is highly subjective, then how we think about creativity at work, where tasks and goals need to be objectified and quantified, is especially tricky. Fortunately, there are a few ways organizations can lay a foundation that encourages the kinds of creativity that may yield higher levels of practical, working happiness.

The importance of what Tom Harbeck experienced at Chiat-Day, and what I experienced when I was part of the team starting *Spy* magazine—that sense of being on a difficult and slightly scary but essentially thrilling *mission*—is corroborated by scholarly research that supports the positive-psychology premise that we sometimes need challenge and ambiguity to make the positives more meaningful. A study conducted in 2006 by Christina Ting Fong, an assistant professor at the University of Washington Business School, suggests that the optimal state for an individual seeking maximum creativity at work is to embrace an in-between emotional state, neither happy-go-luckily complacent nor anxiously stressed-out. After asking college students to write about experiences that had made them feel happy, sad, neutral, or ambivalent, she then had them complete something called the Remote Associates Test, a word-association test used to measure creativity. Fong found that those who reported feeling emotionally ambivalent performed significantly better on the creativity test—and believes that it was the presence of mixed emotions that stimulated unconventional, more creative associations.

On the other hand, Willibald Ruch, a psychology professor at the University of Zurich, has experimental findings suggesting that purely positive states are perhaps even more beneficial than ambivalent ones for stimulating creativity. He says that "people who maintain positive emotions have a longer attention span and are more creative in problem-solving and are more open to alternative solutions." And Barbara Fredrickson, a psychologist at the University of North Carolina at Chapel Hill and the author of *Positivity,* has detected a similar effect. In 2005 she conducted a series of experiments in which she showed people video clips designed to elicit emotions that were variously positive (amusement via penguins frolicking, or contentment via scenes of nature), neutral (images of sticks), and negative (scenes of trauma). She found that those who saw the positively charged emotional scenes visually processed the *entire* scene, while the viewers of unpleasant scenes focused on details. Furthermore, she discovered a correlation between the positive emotions and an increased level of brain activity that encouraged the participant to problem-solve in creative ways. She says, in other words, that emotionally negative content tended to produce a more constrained, narrowed focus, while positive feelings stimulated areas in the brain that literally broaden the field of vision. The positive feelings, she found, cause "increases in brain dopamine levels, particularly in the prefrontal cortex and anterior cingulate cortex, which are thought to underlie better cognitive performance." This is not surprising considering the role of the prefrontal cortices in working memory, attention, and cognitive control. As Fredrickson puts it, "Positive emotions . . . open our minds and hearts." She also suggests that there is an optimal ratio—"three positive emotions to lift us up for every negative emotion that drags us down." Furthermore, unlike negative emotions, which narrow options and tend to spur a quick-action response to minimize a specific proximate threat, Fredrickson also corroborated earlier experimental findings that positive emotions were more enduring and expansive—rippling out like circles from a stone dropped in water, enlarging their field of influence.

A positive emotional tenor in real-life workplaces can, it seems, have real, quantifiable consequences. Sigal Barsade, the Wharton School of Business expert on workplace emotions mentioned earlier, says her research has found that on an individual level, positive moods prompt "more flexible decision-making and wider search behavior and greater analytic precision," and suggests that on an organizational level, positive work cultures are "more willing to engage in risky ventures, more accepting of minority opinions and more willing to use decentralized control." Authentically upbeat moods can stimulate creativity, and creativity effectively harnessed can in turn sustain those good moods. And some places are simply better than others when it comes to setting the stage for happiness at work.

Because happiness, like laughter, has a distinctly viral aspect, it stands to reason that it can be cultivated by organizations. In 2008, Nicholas Christakis, a physician and sociologist at Harvard, and James Fowler, a political scientist at the University of California San Diego, published a fascinating study in the *British Medical Journal* showing that "social networks have clusters of happy and unhappy people within them that reach out to three degrees of separation. . . . A person's happiness is related to the happiness of their friends, and their friends' friends, and their friends' friends' friends—that is, to people well beyond their social horizon." In other words, as Christakis and Fowler put it, "happiness . . . is not merely a function of personal experience, but also is a property of groups." And thus "good behaviors," as a *New York Times Magazine* article about the study put it, "like quitting smoking or staying slender or being happy pass from friend to friend almost as if they were a contagious virus . . . and the same is true of bad behaviors—clusters of friends appeared to 'infect' each other with obesity, unhappiness and smoking."

Wharton professor Sigal Barsade also has data suggesting that an emotional *affinity* among members of management teams is highly important—regardless of gender and regardless of how emotionally "intelligent" or "unintelligent" a company's managers happen to be. In a study she conducted in 2000 of 239 top managers at sixty-two U.S. companies, she discovered that "financial performance is greater if the management team has similar personalities." Workplaces are confined social-network petri dishes. Presumably attitudes and behaviors—for better as well as worse—can be contagiously modeled at least as powerfully at work as through Facebook, MySpace, and Twitter. And if, like the 46 percent of our Emotional Incidents in the Workplace respondents who had *not* experienced *any* moments of happiness at work during the past year, you find that you are in the market for a little bit more joy in your life, you might think about seeking out those colleagues at work who seem to have more fun or radiate more contentment.

A study of business teams conducted by the journal *American Behavior Science* supports this notion, finding that work teams in relatively better moods produced higher profits for their companies and reported higher customer-satisfaction ratings. Richard Davidson, a professor of psychology and psychiatry at the University of Wisconsin, says that positive emotions encourage what my dad used to call stick-to-it-iveness. According to Davidson, some studies demonstrate that "the stronger the activation in the left frontal lobe"—that is, the area in the brain implicated in problem-solving and certain kinds of reasoning—"the more there are certain positive emotions, such as vigor, zeal, and persistence." According to a survey in *Psychological Bulletin,* happier people miss fewer days of work, and what boss doesn't want to encourage that?

Ed Diener, a University of Illinois psychologist mentioned earlier in this chapter, takes this idea a step further, suggesting that happiness, while not essential to survival, is nevertheless a desirable evolutionary trait, and that happier people tend to be more successful. In a paper co-authored with Sonja Lyubomirsky and Laura King, Diener writes that data derived from several studies "reveals that happy workers enjoy multiple advantages over their less happy peers. Individuals high in subjective well-being are more likely to secure job interviews, to be evaluated more positively by supervisors once they obtain a job, to show superior performance and productivity, and to handle managerial jobs better. They are also less likely to show counterproductive workplace behavior and job burnout. Even before entering the workforce, people with high subjective well-being are more likely to graduate from college. Furthermore, happy individuals appear to secure 'better' jobs." But it doesn't just stop with getting a better job. "Once a happy person obtains a job, he or she is more likely to succeed. Employees high in dispositional positive affect receive relatively more favorable evaluations from supervisors and others." And employment in more desirable jobs with better performance reviews results, according to Diener, in the happy people earning more money.

BUILDING YOUR CREATIVITY EMOTION MANAGEMENT TOOLKIT

So how does one *manage* all this touchy-feely stuff? One doesn't budget for happiness, or set quotas for flow experiences and comic moments. Here a few approaches to consider.

EMT—MANAGING CREATIVITY

Management of the creative process, according to Tom Harbeck, "is not about laying down absolute laws. It's not a science, but more about how you get there. What you learn and discover *dur-*

ing the process is incredibly important to coming up with the solution. The whole be-here-now mindfulness approach is central to nurturing creativity. But that's hard to quantify and justify to others who are waiting for the new look or the great tagline or whatever the brief promised." It turns out that taking time along the journey to let the work unfold is essential to making sure you not only arrive at the destination but also arrive at the destination with quality work.

"It's a lot easier to *react* to something than to *create* it," says Tom. And this is where a lot of emotional tension—where the perception of work is so subjective and almost impossible to quantify—arises in the workplace. "Almost without fail there's any number of people who will say, 'I could have done that,' or say, as if annoyed, 'Why'd you make it *green*?' And they've totally dismissed the process that went into creating a marketing campaign, an ad, or a logo." Tom has three rules that facilitate discussion of creative work, and they calm what is often a tense process.

Rule #1: "*Anybody can say anything about the work at any time.* From the newest assistant to the visitor in the lobby, feel free to comment."

Rule #2: "*While you can say anything, you must be sensitive.* It's simply stupid to say that you think something sucks after it's been shipped and you watched it go out the door. Or to roll your eyes and say 'Why in the world would you put the logo *there*?' "

Rule #3: "*You have to give reasons.* You cannot just say 'I don't like it, it's no good.' It can be 'Because women don't like bald eagles,' but there has to be a reason, so that the creative people are prepared to listen, more open to whatever they hear, and better able to take in what they can use."

Anne Sweeney, the president of Disney/ABC TV, has a somewhat different approach to managing creative people. "I think emotion is critical to the creation of content. I love people who unabashedly tap into their inner lives, because the people who dig deepest into their personal stories come up with the best things." And since emotion is critical to creativity, how to manage the inevitable emotional fireworks? Anne has found that "if you put any conflict back into the context of the story—if you keep going back to the story and keep asking how it fits into the story—you can usually resolve what's going on beneath the surface. There will always be challenging personalities to deal with. I've found [that] the most effective way to manage is to be completely honest and communicate constantly. If you can identify and isolate the hot spot, you can contain and resolve it, so everyone can keep moving forward."

EMT—NURTURING YOUR OWN CREATIVITY

There are many paths to take to tap into your creative self, but artist and author Maira Kalman once shared with me one of the easiest and most helpful. Her premise is that if you never take the time to open yourself to the world and fill your creative well, you will eventually run out of ideas. It's Daniel Gilbert's variety principle in action, but once again something most of us forget to do with any regularity. Kalman spends a lot of time simply wandering around when she visits other cities, observing, talking to strangers, walking into odd stores, taking pictures, thinking, inhaling the rich diversity of unfamiliar life. To many people it would appear that Kalman was meandering unproductively, wasting time, and avoiding actual work. But for her, spending a few hours immersed in a new community, processing all the sensory stimuli, is crucial fuel for her creative process. Without it, she would have none of her museum exhibitions, bestselling books, or iconic wristwatches. A narrow range of input results in the same narrow range of output. I've often said about executives who spend their whole working lives hermetically sealed—getting into chauffeur-driven town cars, going into meetings in office buildings, and returning to those town cars and their own office buildings—that there is no way they can evaluate the originality of a new project or properly understand their customers if they exist only in that kind of bubble. In most fields, innovation *needs* to be informed and sometimes provoked by the unpredictable hurly-burly of messy, surprising real life.

TWELVE

We May Have Come from Mars and Venus, but We All Live on Earth

There can be no knowledge without emotion. We may be aware of a truth, yet until we have felt its force, it is not ours. To the cognition of the brain must be added the experience of the soul. —Arnold Bennett

HOW GETTING REAL ABOUT EMOTION COULD TRANSFORM THE WAY WORK WORKS

The goal of organizations should not be to *eliminate* the expression of negative emotions at work, which is what a certain kind of corporate human resources paradigm endeavors to do. We are Captain Kirks and Dr. McCoys, Spouters and Believers, most of us, as much as or more than we are Solver-like Mr. Spocks. For a particular individual in a particular job situation, negative emotion can be the source of renewed energy, as an angry she-doesn't-get-me-so-I'll-show-*her* prod to excellence, or as a fearful our-sales-are-tanking concentration of the mind, or as an anxious what-are-the-chances-that-disaster-could-happen reality check.

If a person fails to do her job well and feels pain as a result, the negative feeling should operate as a catalyst for stepping up her game.

The goal of any person or organization should be to allow emotion at work, in all of its gendered nuances, its *due*—but not to excess. Again, as with most of life, it's a Goldilocks and the Three Bears calibration question—you want not too soft or too hard, not too cold or too hot, but the elusive "just right." After doing the research for this book, my strong sense is that very few workplaces have their emotional temperatures set anything close to just right—rather, that they are way too cold or way too hot or swing wildly from one extreme to the other. And that, I think, despite universal lip-service acknowledgment of "emotional intelligence," is because paying careful, systematic attention to emotion has been considered beyond the scope of managers and the managed, too personal, too intangible, implicitly sexist, essentially off-limits.

I've mainly discussed two evolutionary functions of emotion—to protect the individual from harm and to promote the advancement of the group and species. Work is the most significant modern environment where both kinds of emotions—*I want more money and status to optimize my survival, we work together so the group thrives*—are in perpetual interplay. And we are, tens of thousands of years into this human project, still in the process of adopting and adapting new behavioral rules that reflect life at the desk or the video screen or among consumers rather than lives as hunters or, more recently, farmers, artisans, and laborers.

Understanding the truths that neuroscience is revealing will allow us greater awareness and thus control of the emotions that shape our decisions and behavior at work. Learning and paying attention to what motivates us and in what measure—anger, anxiety, fear, happiness—can help us learn to manage and use those emotions more effectively.

WHERE ARE WE HEADED?

If insights from developing neuroscience research coupled with gender-balanced workplaces are leading to a new openness about what constitutes appropriate behavior on the job, other more structural factors are also influencing workplace interactions. In the twentieth century it was easy to compartmentalize (rational) work life and (emotional) home life, but today our information economy and technology have made work more portable than ever. Because the twenty-first-century workplace is no longer always strictly a specific place where people go, away from their homes—work happens at home, at the airport, in the car, at the coffee shop, or wherever—it is no longer clear how we should manage our emotions in such a fluid social landscape.

The membranes between work and private life are porous, with employers and employees often expecting mutually interdependent accessibility and accountability almost 24/7. Our children and spouses can reach us electronically throughout the official workday. And private behavior can instantly reverberate at work through social networking platforms. One public relations executive I know was recently fired after he tweeted disparagingly about one of his client's hometowns. Others fire off retaliatory e-mails late at night only to regret their tone and intent in the cold light of day. Facebook friends from work can stumble on compromising pictures from a bachelor party. Anonymous mobile uploads can instantly broadcast unflattering emotional displays of surly customer service employees or misbehaving CEOs. And the more we relegate communication to the electronic realm, the greater our longing for human contact. The rule book for modern office etiquette has yet to be codified. How do we avoid hurting one another's feelings if everything is supposed to be transparent and accessible? How can others understand the emotion behind what we're trying to say in an e-mail? What are the lines that should not be crossed?

Further muddying our traditional boundaries and protocols is the less rigidly hierarchical workplace ethos. The greater "flatness" within organizations, the blending of the playful with the practical, jeans and T-shirts as everyday office attire, and Ping-Pong during breaks—all of that seems here to stay. And unlike the "open" office plans of the sixties that were organized along rigid factory-floor-like grids, where the most junior employees were closest to the elevator banks and the most senior employees occupied fortified corner spaces, modern open-office architecture is supposed to eschew the grid in favor of a more organic flow—employees are scattered about and meeting rooms and "conversation pods" are woven throughout. Fewer doors, less privacy, and glass enclosures have forced a greater transparency that brings the emotional life of an office into the foreground. As the CEO sees the mail clerk doing his rounds, so, too, can the assistant manager keep closer tabs on the actions and moods of the executive vice president. People at all levels of an organization receive copies of e-mails.

Although conventional wisdom might suggest that more horizontal organizations automatically promote easy, authentic, hang-loose emotional expression, Jeffrey Sonnenfeld, a Yale School of Management professor and leadership expert, begs to differ. "Flat cultures are flat only to the publicists and the titans who run the companies. Those in the ranks know that 'lateral' communities remain hierarchical. These new structures create a whole new level of inequities that are harder to manage than a bureaucracy. Within 'flat' organizations, there is the same amount of cronyism and rank, it's just a lot harder to figure out what's going on. There are no clear processes for resource allocation or decision-making." If anything, nominally flatter organizations tend to require even higher levels of emotional competency and more emotional effort to navigate the amorphous command structures.

And throughout it all, no one knows exactly how they are supposed to act. Should we high-five an underling? Is it cool to make jokes with the boss? What if the woman in the next cubicle overhears us crying?

Clear rules for the new world simply don't exist. But it may be that women's biologically driven inclination to collaborate lends itself best to this amorphous new circumstance. Years ago, Judy Rosener, a professor emerita at the University of California, conducted a study of seminal male and female leaders for The International Women's Forum and found that men and women described their leadership and its effectiveness in very different ways. According to Rosener, the men viewed their job performance as more transactional in nature—"as a series of transactions with subordinates—exchanging rewards for services rendered or punishment for inadequate performance . . . [and] the men are also more likely to use power that comes from their organizational position and formal authority." Women, on the other hand, described their leadership style as more "transformational—getting subordinates to transform their own self-interest into the interest of the group through concern for the broader goal. Moreover, they ascribed their power to personal characteristics like charisma, interpersonal skills, hard work, or personal contacts rather than to organizational stature." Rosener was among the first to champion women's collaborative styles, and concluded that the ways in which women share information and power encourages a level of personal participation that in turn lets a greater number of people feel powerful and personally invested in the ongoing success of their companies than is the case in more competitive workplaces. As McKinsey &

Company, a management consulting firm, discovered in a 2007 study, *Women Matter: Female Leadership, a Competitive Edge for the Future,* there is a clear link between management performance and the presence of women in management teams. Women's leadership practices, McKinsey declared, will be "critical in meeting the expected challenges companies will face over the coming years." McKinsey used a proprietary diagnostic tool to identify nine key leadership behaviors: "participative decision making," "role model," "inspiration," "expectations and rewards," "people development," "intellectual stimulation," "efficient communication," "individualistic decision making," and "control and corrective action." The study found that "while men and women apply all nine leadership behaviors, they do so with different frequencies" and that four of the key behaviors—intellectual stimulation, inspiration, participative decision-making, and expectations and rewards (in other words, those areas in which women tend to excel)—were deemed by both women and men the most critical to the success of a company.

These insights matter for two reasons. First, the hardest-hit major industries in the recent recession—manufacturing, construction, and finance—are also the most male-dominated sectors; the great majority of the eight million Americans who've lost their jobs since 2007 are men. This served to increase the female fraction of the survivors *and* prompted married, nonworking women to enter the working world. This is why women now, as previously noted, suddenly make up the majority of the U.S. labor force. Second, America's transformation into a postindustrial, information-centric, service-oriented economy and culture continues apace. More than 60 percent of American jobs are now professional, managerial, administrative, or sales-based, while less than 25 percent are in manufacturing, construction, extraction, or transportation. Over the next few decades, jobs will grow in education, health care, and elder care—jobs that have traditionally been the domain of women, in part because they harness women's native empathy and other emotional-intelligence skills.

THE NEXT WAVE

For a century or two, we were a society and culture where the workplace, dominated by men, was a venue in which emotions, those inconvenient things, were constrained, suppressed, denied, and hidden. That's changed. But we haven't yet arrived at the next stage of equilibrium, where people have a sure sense of how they should or can express and respond to emotions in the public realm, especially that peculiarly intimate-yet-public realm of the workplace. I think America and Americans are also still figuring out and coming to grips with our post-sixties era: it was a very big bang that happened just four decades ago, after all, with female emancipation *and* a new definition of happiness (do your own thing, let it all hang out, follow your bliss) both gaining momentum at once. We're still in the aftermath, still piecing together a new paradigm that makes sense and feels right.

Because it's women's economic lives that have changed the most quickly, and because we are, yes, more overtly emotional, women are still at sea about how we're supposed to behave and how we are regarded in this (still) new era of working women. Women and men continue to think quite differently about what these changes mean. In this somewhat topsy-turvy post-women's-revolution age, it may be *female* more than male attitudes that inhibit the establishment of new, looser norms. A 2009 *Time* magazine poll reported that two thirds of working women believe that men resent powerful women. And yet according to the same poll, an astonishing 75 percent of men believe something like the opposite—that women no longer need to behave more like men to be taken seriously in the workplace. What this suggests to me is that while women have mostly won the war for parity in men's minds, they have yet to allow themselves to believe it. And by not believing it, they restrain themselves from acting in more naturally emotional, unself-consciously female ways that would let them be happier.

Perri Peltz has experienced this kind of dilemma firsthand, first in 1996, when she was working for WNBC News in New York City. Only five months after giving birth to her first child, she discovered that she was pregnant again. She remembers hiding the second pregnancy for as long as she could because she was afraid of the network's reaction. "But the interesting thing," she says, "was the response of my news director once he found out. He sat me down and said, 'This is what makes up the humanity of our news organization and we embrace it,' and he could not have been more gracious or understanding." In spite of this tolerant environment, though, she still had an old-school fear of asking for special treatment for a family matter. In 2007, when she was anchoring the evening news broadcast for WNBC, she once again faced the kind of life-balance choice all working parents do. Her son played baseball during her broadcast, and she wanted to make at least one game of his season. As she was finagling to come up with some excuse to leave, her news director approached her, saying, "We will go out of our way to make sure that you can go to a game. It's my job to make it happen for you." Now, few of us are stars like Perri, for whom management might bend over backward, but I do believe her experience is nevertheless indicative of a new attitude throughout the workplace to try to accommodate work/family balance issues.

In spite of these heartening anecdotes suggesting that we're moving toward real gender equality at work, data from the U.S. General Social Survey and *The Paradox of Declining Female Happiness* study conducted in 2009 by Professors Betsey Stevenson and Justin Wolfers at the Wharton School of Business suggest that women's overall happiness has *dropped* consistently since 1972, regardless of income, health, or marital status. It may be that in aggregate, happiness and job-market parity really have been zero-sum (or worse) for women, that the personal emotional price of modern economic independence—that is, putting up with the stresses and anxieties of the workplace—is higher than we care to admit.

Simultaneously, men are facing unprecedented shifts in their social and economic positions. Teresa Ghilarducci, the director of the Schwartz Center for Economic Policy Analysis at the New School for Social Research, has written extensively about how U.S. men are on a downwardly mobile path long-term. While women over the last thirty years have seen their average pay increase by about half, men's income has been flat. Men today expect to do worse financially than their grandfathers did, while women expect to do better than their grandmothers did. This change in status for men, especially in a society where one's identity is so closely aligned with one's income, is a gigantic shift that has barely begun. We are at a moment of powerful convergence, when women's *rising* expectations are meeting men's *sinking* expectations. But perhaps where there is flux of this magnitude there is also opportunity.

In my research for this book I talked to dozens of women in their twenties and early thirties, and I'm convinced that this generation, which wasn't even alive during the era of outright male domination, really does embody a new force not so burdened by the post-feminist-revolution confusions, fears, and overcompensations. They wear their feminism lightly, unself-consciously or even unconsciously. I'm hopeful that as they and their younger sisters move into and through the workforce, and as older workers begin to retire, the evolution I've described and encouraged in this book will accelerate. And because a generation of men has grown up working with women by their side from day one, young men no longer find women at work an anomaly. A greater acceptance of emotional range for women and men on the job can be part and parcel of a new American heyday.

If you, like me, have a sense that the United States—as a nation and a society, politically, economically, and culturally—has arrived at one of its periodic sink-or-swim moments, I hope you'll also agree that a greater tolerance for emotional expressiveness for both women and men in the workplace is among the tools that can help us regain our footing. With so much economic upheaval and creative destruction under way, there are potentially unprecedented opportunities for organizational behavior to positively evolve. We have arrived at a historical point where the collective desire for Americans to get our mojo back has coincided with the emergence of a more refined scientific understanding of human behavior. And that offers us a chance to redefine American enterprise for the twenty-first century, to rethink the way work works.

I suggest that if men and women were to express more emotion at work routinely and easily—jokes, warmth, sadness, anger, tears, all of it—then as a people we might not implode emotionally so frequently, or feel the need to gawk at others emoting in inappropriate ways. If we can openly acknowledge our gender-based biological and neurological differences, we can feel freer to tackle whatever challenges we face at full capacity. In almost every era and culture, as producers and creators and workers, as economic actors, the genders have always worked as a kind of tag team. The balance has changed in the last few years, but the tag-team model can still work, perhaps better than ever. Both genders can win by granting the other—and, for women, fellow females—a greater range of expressiveness on the job. And women and men can both be freed to bring their full, true selves to the game. Isn't it time for us all to get a lot more rational about emotion? The prospect of that happening makes me so happy I could cry.

Conversations for Building Emotional Intelligence

A DISCUSSION GUIDE

If you liked my book and would like to expand your tool kit for developing greater resiliency, invite your friends to join you in conversation. Each person will bring a fresh perspective and new insight into the emotional complexities we all face at work. The questions below will help you tailor the discussion to suit your needs.

1. What motivates you on the job? Explore factors such as good pay, company mission, being acknowledged for your work, relationships with colleagues you can trust, and reasonable hours. How do you prioritize these intangibles?

2. Does humor play in the workplace? Describe how you might use it to navigate a work situation. What do you see as the advantages and disadvantages of this strategy?

3. Does emotion play a role in creativity? Are there things that management can do to encourage more creativity? What stops you from feeling innovative?

4. Working from home is emotionally different from working in an office or other kind of face-to-face environment. What are the emotional challenges of each situation?

5. Do you think different personality types handle emotions differently? What are the implications for this?

6. Have you ever had an "Aha!" epiphany moment of emotional self-understanding? What was it? What kind of change did it initiate for you?

7. How would you like to be smarter about handling your own emotions?

8. Can you think of a situation when you cried at work? Do you know what triggered your tears? Were there issues outside of work that you feel influenced how you behaved? Try to specifically name how you felt immediately before the tears, while you were crying, and afterward. Does looking at the episode through this emotional lens clarify the event? Would you change your behavior, how and why?

9. If you were with others, what do you think they thought? Consider talking to the person(s) to see if what you believe they thought is accurate.

10. Has someone ever cried in front of you at work? What did you think or do? Do you think you judge others for displaying emotion at work more or less than yourself?

11. What if it was a man crying? Does gender influence your perception? If it does, analyze what this means to your work environment.

12. Has anyone ever yelled at you at work? Describe the situation and how you felt. Were you able to talk with others about the situation?

13. Do you think a double standard exists that allows bosses to get angry but not regular workers or that views angry men and women differently?

14. Is there a cost to getting angry where you work? Is there a cost for crying at work?

15. Have you ever felt boiling mad at work? What triggered the feeling and what did you do? How did you feel afterward whether or not you exploded? If you did explode, what steps did you take to manage the impact of your outburst?

16. Think about a recent highly charged emotional work episode and analyze it through the brain science and neurology discussed in this book. How does knowing about how your biology really works help to clarify and/or change your experience of the situation?

17. Have you ever felt physically or emotionally afraid on the job? Describe the circumstances and what you did about them.

18. How often do you feel anxious at work? Are the triggers related to work or home life? Does the anxiety relate to your skills (or lack thereof) or to what is known as "the imposter

syndrome?" Does your anxiety get in the way of your productivity or advancement? Discuss strategies you might use to lessen your anxiety.

19. Do you feel like you no longer have any personal time? Is this because of your boss's/job's expectations or your own? Using some of the ideas you've encountered in this book—and using some of your own—create several tactics to give yourself more free time.

20. How important do you think the culture of an organization is in shaping how employees act?

21. Is there a generational difference in the way people express emotion and behave on the job?

22. Are there varying rules for how men and women can act in the workplace? Does one gender have it "better" at work? Explore why that is and how you could change the environment to alter those dynamics.

23. Describe how you think successful people behave in the workplace. Does successful leadership require compassion and empathy, the ability to be steely and tough? Can a person be a terrific leader without some of those qualities?

24. Can compassion influence the bottom line of an organization? If so, how?

25. What happens in organizations when management rewards people who display bad behavior with the excuse that "they do good work" or are "our most productive players?"

Acknowledgments

A few years ago at a cocktail party, Sara Levinson, a colleague from my MTV Network days, threw out a casual comment about women who cry at work. That germ grew into this book. A legion of others helped and supported me. Without Gerry Laybourne's generous leap of faith in hiring me at Nickelodeon, I'd have never acquired the experience or perspective necessary to write this book. Her wisdom and guidance kept me as sane as I could be when I worked with her. Without Priscilla Painton's initial encouragement I might never have tackled such a richly complicated subject. Thank you, Ruth Liebmann, for brainstorming ideas with me before there was a proposal, let alone a book. Thanks to my agent, Suzanne Gluck, who was her usual smart and enthusiastic force-of-nature self. Thanks to the team at Random House—Gina Centrello, Jane von Mehren, Jennifer Hershey, Sally Marvin, and Tom Perry—who got the idea instantly. Jane von Mehren is an amazing editor, the kind they're not supposed to make anymore, and she and Kerri Buckley helped me turn my scribblings into prose. I bow at your feet. Thanks also to Avideh Bashirrad, Andrea Sheehan, Robbin Schiff, Penelope

Haynes, Theresa Zoro, Carol Schneider, Brian McClendon, London King, and Ashley Gratz-Collier, who made the book "real."

Carla Hendra, my advertising fairy godsister, paved the way for me at J. Walter Thompson, which became my indispensable partner. JWT's Rosemarie Ryan and William Charnock are the kind of enlightened executives who make me hopeful about the future of American business. If not for Mark Truss, JWT's Zen master of research, this book would be a much lesser creation. Thanks also to Greg Weiss, Yusuf Chuku, Merrie Harris, and the rest of the team at JWT.

A special thanks goes to Dr. Paul Browde, a game and gracious man who partnered with me step-by-step in a challenging process. Daniela Schiller made neuroscience accessible and Candace Raio checked its accuracy, while Victoria Brescoll, Jeff Sonnenfeld, Kerry Sulkowicz, Isabelle Anderson, and Sigal Barsade gave me great insight into emotion in business. Daniel Goleman, Howard Gardner, and Dan Ariely gave me the benefit of their wisdom. Joanne Gruber helped me above and beyond the call of duty. And to each of you hundreds out there who gave me your time and insight in lengthy interviews, I thank you.

My kitchen cabinet—David Andersen, Erika Andersen, Kristi Andersen, Andrea Barnet, Emily Berry, Akiko Busch, Stephen Chao, Jenny Douglas, Cathy Hamilton, John Heilemann, Maira Kalman, Barbara Kass, Danica Kombol, Susanne Moore, Elise O'Shaughnessy, Diana Rhoten, Michael Rips, Margaret Roach, and Linda Schupack—I am blessed to count you as friends, and your wisdom helped shape both me and this book. I don't know what I'd do without you. Thank you, sister Jane, for putting up with my emotional highs and lows and for providing ballast my entire life. And thank you, Kurt, Lucy, and Kate for being the best family ever.

Bibliography

Ariely, Dan. *Predictably Irrational: The Hidden Forces That Shape Our Decisions.* New York, NY: Harper, 2008.

Ashkanasy, Neal M., Charmine Härtel, and W. J. Zerbe. *Emotions in the Workplace: Research, Theory, and Practice.* Westport, CT: Quorum, 2000.

Averill, James. *Anger and Aggression: An Essay on Emotion.* New York, NY: Springer-Verlag, 1982.

Babcock, Linda, and Sara Laschever. *Ask for It: How Women Can Use the Power of Negotiation to Get What They Really Want.* New York, NY: Bantam Dell, 2008.

Barsade, Sigal G. *The Ripple Effect: Emotional Contagion and Its Influence on Group Behavior.* Johnson Graduate School, Cornell University, 2002.

Barsade, Sigal G., and Olivia A. O'Neill. "Affective Culture in Organizations: Its Influence in the Long-term Care Setting." *Science Quarterly* (2009).

Barsade, Sigal G., Andrew J. Ward, Jean D. F. Turner, and Jeffrey A. Sonnenfeld. *To Your Heart's Content: A Model of Affective Diversity in Top Management Teams.* Cornell University, 2000.

Bateson, Mary Catherine. *Composing a Life.* New York, NY: Grove, 2001.

Begley, Sharon. *Train Your Mind, Change Your Brain: How a New Science Reveals Our Extraordinary Potential to Transform Ourselves.* New York, NY: Ballantine, 2007.

Bly, Robert. *Iron John: A Book about Men.* Reading, MA: Addison-Wesley, 1990.

Booth, Rebecca. *The Venus Week.* Philadelphia, PA: Da Capo, 2008.

The Bottom Line: Connecting Corporate Performance and Gender Diversity. New York, NY: Catalyst, 2004.

Brescoll, Victoria, and Eric Uhlmann. "Can an Angry Woman Get Ahead?" *Psychological Science* 19 (2008).

Brizendine, Louann. *The Female Brain.* New York, NY: Broadway, 2006.

Brizendine, Louann. *The Male Brain.* New York, NY: Broadway, 2010.

Bronson, Po. *What Should I Do with My Life?* New York, NY: Random House, 2002.

Burnham, Terry. *Mean Markets and Lizard Brains: How to Profit from the New Science of Irrationality.* Hoboken, NJ: John Wiley & Sons, 2005.

Cahill, Larry. "Why Sex Matters for Neuroscience." *Nature Reviews Neuroscience* (2006).

Carroll, Michael. *Awake at Work: Facing the Challenges of Life on the Job.* Boston, MA: Shambhala, 2004.

Christakis, Nicholas A., and James H. Fowler. *Connected: The Surprising Power of Our Social Networks and How They Shape Our Lives.* New York, NY: Little, Brown, 2009.

Clancy, Pauline Rose, and Suzanne Imes. "The Imposter Phenomenon in High Achieving Women: Dynamics and Therapeutic Intervention." *Psychotherapy, Theory, Research and Practice* 15.3 (1978).

Coates, J. M., and J. Herbert. "Endogenous Steroids and Financial Risk Taking on a London Trading Floor." *PNAS—National Academy of Sciences of the United States of America* 105 (2008).

Cole, Joni B., and B. K. Rakhra. *Water Cooler Diaries: Women Across America Share Their Day at Work.* New York, NY: Da Capo, 2008.

Coughlin, Linda, Ellen Wingard, and Keith Hollihan. *Enlightened Power: How Women Are Transforming the Practice of Leadership.* San Francisco, CA: Jossey-Bass, 2005.

Csikszentmihalyi, Mihaly. *Flow: The Psychology of Optimal Experience.* New York, NY: Harper Perennial, 2008.

Cummings, E. Mark, Carolyn Zahn-Waxler, and Marian Radke-Yarrow. *National Institute of Health, Child Development.* Rep. Ann Arbor, MI: Society for Research in Child Development, 1981.

Damasio, Antonio R. *Descartes' Error: Emotion, Reason, and the Human Brain.* New York, NY: Putnam, 1994.

Darwin, Charles. *The Origin of Species.* Ware, U.K.: Wordsworth Editions, 1998.

Diener, E., and M. Seligman. "Very Happy People." *Psychological Science* 13 (2002).

DiSesa, Nina. *Seducing the Boys Club: Uncensored Tactics from a Woman at the Top.* New York, NY: Ballantine, 2008.

Eagly, Alice Hendrickson, and Linda Lorene Carli. *Through the Labyrinth: The Truth about How Women Become Leaders.* Boston, MA: Harvard Business School, 2007.

Eliot, Lise. "The Truth about Boys and Girls." *Scientific American Mind* (May–June 2010).

Fabes, Richard, and Carol Martin. "Gender and Age: Stereotypes of Emotionality." *Personality and Social Psychology Bulletin* (1991).

Farrell, Warren. *The Myth of Male Power: Why Men Are the Disposable Sex.* New York: Simon & Schuster, 1993.

Fell, Joseph P. *Emotion in the Thought of Sartre.* New York, NY: Columbia University Press, 1965.

Fisher, Helen E. *The First Sex: The Natural Talents of Women and How They Are Changing the World.* New York, NY: Random House, 1999.

Fong, Christina Ting. "The Effects of Emotional Ambivalence on Creativity." *Academy of Management Journal* 49 (2006).

Frankel, Lois P. *Nice Girls Don't Get the Corner Office: 101 Unconscious Mistakes Women Make That Sabotage Their Careers.* New York, NY: Warner Business, 2004.

Frankl, Viktor Emil. *Man's Search for Meaning.* New York, NY: Washington Square/Pocket, 1985.

Fredrickson, Barbara. *Positivity.* New York, NY: Crown, 2009.

Gallagher, Winifred. *Rapt: Attention and the Focused Life.* New York, NY: Penguin, 2009.

Gardner, Howard. *Five Minds for the Future.* Boston, MA: Harvard Business School, 2008.

Gibbs, Nancy. "What Women Want Now." *Time,* October 26, 2009.

Gilbert, Daniel Todd. *Stumbling on Happiness.* New York, NY: Knopf, 2006.

Gladwell, Malcolm. *Outliers: The Story of Success.* New York, NY: Little, Brown, 2008.

Goleman, Daniel. *Destructive Emotions: How Can We Overcome Them?: A Scientific Dialogue with the Dalai Lama.* New York, NY: Bantam, 2004.

Goleman, Daniel. *Emotional Intelligence.* New York, NY: Bantam, 1995.

Goleman, Daniel. *Working with Emotional Intelligence.* New York, NY: Bantam, 1998.

Gray, John. *Men Are from Mars, Women Are from Venus: A Practical Guide for Improving Communication and Getting What You Want in Your Relationships.* New York, NY: HarperCollins, 1992.

Gurian, Michael, and Barbara Annis. *Leadership and the Sexes: Using Gender Science to Create Success in Business.* San Francisco, CA: Jossey-Bass, 2008.

Haidt, Jonathan. *The Happiness Hypothesis: Finding Modern Truth in Ancient Wisdom.* New York, NY: Basic, 2006.

Hanson, Janet. *More than 85 Broads: Women Making Career Choices, Taking Risks, and Defining Success on Their Own Terms.* Chicago, IL: McGraw-Hill, 2006.

Hecht, Jennifer Michael. *The Happiness Myth: Why What We Think Is Right Is Wrong: A History of What Really Makes Us Happy.* San Francisco, CA: Harper, 2007.

Helgesen, Sally. *The Web of Inclusion: A New Architecture for Building Great Organizations.* New York, NY: Currency/Doubleday, 1995.

Hendershot, Heather. *Nickelodeon Nation: The History, Politics, and Economics of America's Only TV Channel for Kids.* New York, NY: NYU Press, 2004.

Hirshman, Linda R. *Get to Work: A Manifesto for Women of the World.* New York, NY: Viking, 2006.

Huffington, Arianna Stassinopoulos. *On Becoming Fearless . . . in Love, Work, and Life.* New York, NY: Little, Brown, 2006.

Huffington, Arianna Stassinopoulos. *The Female Woman.* New York, NY: Random House, 1974.

Isen, A. M., K. A. Daubman, and G. P. Nowicki. "Positive Affect Facilitates Creative Problem Solving." *Journal of Personality and Social Psychology* 52 (1987).

Keilisers, L., S. J. Branie, T. Frijins, C. Finkenauer, and W. Meeus. "Gender Differences in Keeping Secrets from Parents in Adolescence." *Developmental Psychology* (2010).

Keirsey, David, and Marilyn M. Bates. *Please Understand Me: Character & Temperament Types.* Del Mar, CA: Distributed by Prometheus Nemesis Book Company, 1984.

Kellerman, Barbara, Deborah L. Rhode, and Sandra Day O'Connor. *Women and Leadership: The State of Play and Strategies for Change.* San Francisco, CA: Jossey-Bass, 2007.

Kimura, Doreen. "Monthly Fluctuations in Sex Hormones Affect Women's Cognitive Skills." *Psychology Today* (November 1989).

Kindlon, Daniel J. *Alpha Girls: Understanding the New American Girl and How She Is Changing the World.* Emmaus, PA: Rodale, 2006.

Kinman, Gail, and Yasmine Yaghmour. "Why Women Cry." Proc. of Annual Conference of the Division of Occupational Psychology. British Psychological Society, 2007.

Kounios, J., J. L. Frymiare, E. M. Bowden, J. I. Fleck, K. Subramaniam, T. B. Parrish, and M. J. Jung-Beeman. "The Prepared Mind: Neural Activity Prior to Problem Presentation Predicts Subsequent Solution by Sudden Insight." *Psychological Science* 17 (2006).

Lehrer, Jonah. *How We Decide.* Boston, MA: Houghton Mifflin Harcourt, 2009.

Leineweber, Constanze, Hugo Westerlund, Tores Theorell, Mika Kivimaki, Peter Westerholm, and Lars Alfredsson. "Covert Coping with Unfair Treatment at Work and Risk of Incident of Myocardial Infarction and Cardiac Death Among Men." *Journal of Epidemiology and Community Health* (2009).

Lerner, Harriet Goldhor. *The Dance of Anger: A Woman's Guide to Changing the Patterns of Intimate Relationships.* New York, NY: Perennial Library, 1986. 2005.

Letherby, Gayle. *Feminist Research in Theory and Practice.* Buckingham, U.K.: Open University Press, 2003.

Lord, Robert G., Richard J. Klimoski, and Ruth Kanfer. *Emotions in the Workplace: Understanding the Structure and Role of Emotions in Organizational Behavior.* San Francisco, CA: Jossey-Bass, 2002.

Lutz, Tom. *Crying: The Natural and Cultural History of Tears.* New York, NY: W.W. Norton, 1999.

Lyubomirsky, S., S. King, and E. Diener. "The Benefits of Frequent Positive Affect." *Psychological Bulletin* 131 (2005).

Masson, J. Moussaieff, and Susan McCarthy. *When Elephants Weep: The Emotional Lives of Animals.* New York, NY: Delacorte, 1995.

McRae, Kateri, Kevin Ochsner, Iris Mauss, John Gabrieli, and James Gross. "Gender Differences in Emotion Regulation: An fMRI Study of Cognitive Reappraisal." *Sage* (2008).

Meyer, Danny. *Setting the Table: The Transforming Power of Hospitality in Business.* New York, NY: HarperCollins, 2006.

Miller, Geoffrey, Joshua M. Tybur, and Brent D. Jordan. "Ovulatory Cycle Effects on Tip Earnings by Lap Dancers: Economic Evidence for Human Estrus?" *Evolution and Human Behavior* (2007).

Pease, Barbara, and Allan Pease. *Why Men Don't Listen & Women Can't Read Maps: How We're Different and What to Do about It.* New York, NY: Welcome Rain, 2000.

Pesuric, A., and W. Bynham. "The New Look in Behavior Modelling." *Training and Development* (1996).

Pink, Daniel H. *A Whole New Mind: Moving from the Information Age to the Conceptual Age.* New York, NY: Riverhead, 2005.

Pinker, Susan. *The Sexual Paradox: Men, Women and the Real Gender Gap.* New York, NY: Scribner, 2008.

Raison, Charles L. "Meditation May Improve Physical and Emotional Responses to Psychological Stress." *Psychoneuroendocrinology* (2008).

Rakel, P., Theresa J. Hoeft, Bruce P. Barrett, Betty A. Chewning, Benjamin M. Craig, and Min Niu. "Practitioner Empathy and the Duration of the Common Cold." *Family Medicine* (2009).

Resnick, Lynda, and Francis Wilkinson. *Rubies in the Orchard: How to Uncover the Hidden Gems in Your Business.* New York, NY: Doubleday, 2009.

Rosener, Judy B. "Ways Women Lead." *Harvard Business Review* (1990).

Rushton, Phillippe J., and Douglas N. Jackson. "Males Have Greater Sex Differences in General Mental Ability from 100,000 17-to-18-Year-Olds on the Scholastic Assessment Test." *Intelligence* 34 (2006).

Salmansohn, Karen. *How to Succeed in Business Without a Penis: Secrets and Strategies for the Working Woman.* New York, NY: Harmony, 1996.

Seligman, Martin E. P. *Authentic Happiness: Using the New Positive Psychology to Realize Your Potential for Lasting Fulfillment.* New York, NY: Free Press, 2004.

Shields, Stephanie A. *Speaking from the Heart: Gender and the Social Meaning of Emotion.* Cambridge, U.K.: Cambridge University Press, 2002.

Shipman, Claire, and Katty Kay. *Womenomics.* New York, NY: HarperCollins, 2009.

Stevenson, Betsey, and Justin Wolfers. "The Paradox of Declining Female Happiness." *American Economic Journal: Economic Policy, American Economic Association* 1(2) (2009).

Sudsuang, Ratree, Vilai Chentanez, and Kongdej Veluvan. "Effect of Buddhist Meditation on Serum Cortisol and Total Protein Levels, Blood Pressure, Pulse Rate, Lung Volume and Reaction Time." *Physiology & Behavior* 50.3 (1991).

Tahmincioglu, Eve. *From the Sandbox to the Corner Office: Lessons Learned on the Journey to the Top.* Hoboken, NJ: Wiley, 2006.

Tannen, Deborah. *You Just Don't Understand: Women and Men in Conversation.* New York: Morrow, 1990.

Tavris, Carol. *Anger: The Misunderstood Emotion.* New York, NY: Simon & Schuster, 1989.

Vance, Erik. "Is Estrogen the New Ritalin?" *Scientific American Mind,* (May–June 2010).

Vincent, Norah. *Self-made Man: One Woman's Year Disguised as a Man.* New York, NY: Penguin, 2006.

Warren, Jane E., Disa A. Sauter, Frank Eisner, Jade Wiland, M. Alexander Dresner, Richard J. S. Wise, Stuart Rosen, and Sophie K. Scott. "Positive Emotions Preferentially Engage an Auditory-Motor 'Mirror' System." *The Journal of Neuroscience* (2006).

Wise, J. *Extreme Fear.* New York, NY: Palgrave Macmillan, 2009.

Wittenbeg-Cox, Avivah, and Alison Maitland. *Why Women Mean Business.* Hoboken, NJ: Wiley, 2009.

Women Matter: Gender Diversity, A Corporate Performance Driver. Rep. New York, NY: McKinsey, 2007.

Zichy, Shoya, and Bonnie Kellen. *Women and the Leadership Q: The Breakthrough System for Achieving Power and Influence.* New York, NY: McGraw-Hill, 2001.

Index

PHOTO: © LUCY ANDERSEN

Anne Kreamer is the author of *It's Always Personal: Navigating Emotion in the Workplace* and *Going Gray: What I Learned about Beauty, Sex, Work, Motherhood, Authenticity, and Everything Else That Really Matters.* She is currently at work on her next book, *Plan C,* about the unprecedented professional adaptability required of everyone in the twenty-first century. She has also worked as a columnist for *Fast Company* and *Martha Stewart Living,* and is a frequent blogger on HarvardBusinessReview.org and NextAvenue.org. Her work has appeared in *Time, The New York Times, The Wall Street Journal, Real Simple,* and *Travel & Leisure.* Previously, she was executive vice president and worldwide creative director for the television channels Nickelodeon and Nick at Nite. She graduated from Harvard College and lives in Brooklyn with her husband, the writer Kurt Andersen.

Anne Kreamer is available for select readings and lectures. To inquire about a possible appearance, please contact the Random House Speakers Bureau at 212-572-2013 or rhspeakers@randomhouse.com.